Pastel Painting Step by Step

PASTEL PAINTING
Step by Step

by Elinor Lathrop Sears

Watson-Guptill Publications · New York

Woman Drying Herself *by Edgar Degas. Courtesy, the Courtauld Institute of Art, London. Degas always preferred casual, action poses to the more formal "studio" poses chosen by most painters of the nude. He often asked his model simply to take a bath and go through the normal actions involved. Then, working at great speed, he would draw the model with rapid strokes. The character of these strokes is evident here.*

Published in the United States of America 1968
by Watson-Guptill Publications
165 West 46 Street, New York, New York
All Rights Reserved.
Printed and Bound in Japan
Library of Congress Catalog Card #68-12402

Contents

4432

Part Two: Demonstrations by Professionals

At the Milliner's *by Edgar Degas. Courtesy, The Metropolitan Museum of Art, Bequest of Mrs. H. O. Havemeyer, 1929. The H. O. Havemeyer Collection. Although Degas' early work is more precise than his later work, the effect is still based on broad masses of color (with little or no smudging) and carefully designed patterns of strokes. In the foreground figure, the chalk is heavily applied, and the strokes dissolve into a crumbly mass on the rough paper. In the background, the vertical strokes are more lightly applied, and the background figure is rendered with a pattern of horizontal, vertical, and diagonal strokes.*

Introduction

This book has been prepared with a threefold objective. First, it has been my primary aim to provide what has long been lacking in America—a complete and exact technical guide to pastel drawing and painting—a working tool, as it were, to place in the hands of the amateur, the student, or the professional artist, so that he may have at his instant command a wealth of information, stated in the simplest terms, telling him precisely how to go about the making of any of the customary types of pastel work.

Meeting the reader's needs

Especially should the book meet the needs of the reader, whether novice or adept, who is turning seriously to pastel for the first time. Starting with a detailed discussion of the necessary supplies and materials—what to get and where to get it—it offers step-by-step demonstrations acquainting the reader with their manifold uses. The instructive text, generously illustrated with reproductions in line, halftone, and full color, leads the reader by easy degrees from such elementary matters as line drawing, tone building, and color manipulation through varied applications of pastel in the representation of still life, landscape, and the human face and figure. Special chapters deal with such subjects as pictorial composition; the combination of pastel with other media; the matting, framing, and preservation of pastels; and pastel diseases, their prevention and cure. Included, too, is a brief history of pastel painting. All of this material is so arranged that the student can utilize it without further assistance.

Personal observations and experiences

Second, it has been my plan to weave into the content of the book as many of my personal observations and experiences as seem to possess general value—the essence of what I have learned during a good many years of intensive activity in the field of pastel. If a recording of some of the things which I have learned proves inspiring and informative to others, I shall be richly rewarded. Also, I have had the temerity to express my views on the vocational aspects of portrait painting in pastel, and I do so here only because it seems an exceptional opportunity to answer certain questions which have been put to me so frequently that it is not unreasonable to assume that they are of general interest.

Reproductions of selected pastels

My third aim is to voice a plea for the more general use of pastel, not only in portraiture—a purpose for which I consider it ideal—but in the representation of all sorts of subject matter. Realizing that the best possible support of my plea lies in the fact that numerous capable artists, past and present, have successfully employed this facile medium, I have included a group of reproductions of selected pastels by some of the greatest of these masters, as well as by some noted contemporaries. I have made no attempt to include *all* the best masters, on the one hand, or the best work of each, on the other; nor is it within my province to venture any appraisal of the relative merits of the examples shown. Rather it has been my plan merely to place before the reader, for his own comparison and study, quite a variety of pastel treatments by artists of different periods and countries.

If you have never drawn before

Some of my readers may be inexperienced in any type of freehand drawing or painting. They may, for example, be unable to depict their subject matter in proper proportion and perspective, or they may be at a loss to discover the correct means of treating values of light and shade, or edges of tone areas. Perhaps they will be bewildered when it comes to the selection or combination of their colors.

In such a case, it might be well for them to postpone their work in pastel until they have mastered the fundamentals of freehand drawing. We are assuming throughout this volume that the reader already knows how to draw his subjects correctly in proportion and perspective, and has at least a fundamental understanding of the treatment of color, and of values of light and shade. (If not, such books as those listed in the Bibliography might prove useful.)

All this has been my aim. At best, there is much that cannot be told with full satisfaction on the printed page, and it is equally evident that no one book can hope to anticipate and meet all the needs of a diversified body of readers. If this book proves of even modest assistance in pointing the way to the pleasure of pastel as a medium, showing the reader an occasional short cut and steering him clear of some of the tedious detours, I shall feel it has justified the time and effort involved.

ELINOR LATHROP SEARS
Lyme, Connecticut

PART ONE
Pastel Techniques

Folk Rock *by Harvey Dinnerstein. Courtesy, Kenmore Galleries, Philadelphia. Working with large, slashing strokes, the artist has dashed in the dominant light and dark tones. The jagged white strokes of the sleeves are particularly striking. Only the face has been drawn in detail. The contours of the right hand are merely indicated, and the left hand consists of carefully placed smudges of color.*

1 / Why Pastel?

Before turning to our how-to-do-it instructions, let us consider some of the possibilities and limitations of pastel as a medium of esthetic expression. Obviously, the virtues of this medium outweigh its faults, or the art would not have enjoyed its long and ever-growing popularity.

Advantages

First, the materials needed are few in number, inexpensive, and readily obtainable. (One can even make many of them if he wishes.) Pastels can be stored in a minimum of space, and cared for with almost no effort. They do not deteriorate with age as oil and watercolor paints so often do.

Second, their mastery, while not to be gained in "six easy lessons," is by no means difficult. A few hours of concentrated experimentation will give one at least an elementary understanding of the basic technical procedures. Progress thereafter will depend largely on the individual. Sooner or later, the student with fair natural aptitude, coupled with reasonable perseverance, will find that his pastels will allow for the production of an astonishing variety of effects.

In fact, we might list as our third attribute of pastels (though it actually stands first in importance) their ability to produce extremely commendable results ranging all the way from rough, quick impressions to highly finished, carefully executed studies.

Range of color effects

As to color, pastels permit a remarkably wide range of light, delicate tints, on the one hand, and, on the other, brilliant, fully saturated hues. Therefore, while pastels are ideally adapted to the expression of quite ethereal effects—no other medium, in fact, can render so sympathetically the subtle lighter colorings of flowers or of human flesh—they are also capable of recording the strongest contrasts of value, or the most strident riot of brilliant color. Another virtue of the pastel medium is that its tones are unusually luminous and alive, with a remarkable degree of scintillation.

Furthermore, this medium permits the artist to record fleeting impressions in a minimum of time. Thus it is ideal for the landscape painter who so often wishes to capture the essence of some ephemeral moment—the bursting of the sun from behind a cloud, the melting mists of early morning, the dash of breaking waves. It is similarly useful in sketching animals and people, where pose and expression are so often transitory. In other words, while pastel is capable of the slowly drawn, slick, super-refined results which certain purposes demand, it is generally at its best for quicker interpretations of a somewhat bolder, more spontaneous nature.

Boldness and simplicity

We can summarize all this by saying that, in technical management, pastel imposes practically no restrictions, no tiresome mannerisms, no tedious processes. Large areas can be covered in a moment with bold, sweeping strokes; significant lines—even fine lines—can be drawn with speed and decision; vibrant colors can be blended directly upon the paper as wanted—a quick whisk of the thumb can reduce a tone to its lowest terms; a touch of stipple or a few rapidly executed strokes can restore life to a dead area, or can raise or lower a value. There is no drying out, as in oils, to rob one's work of its virgin freshness. There is no disturbing shine to the finished product; on the contrary, its matte surface is pleasing when seen in almost any light.

Pastel, too, relates itself with unusual sympathy to its ground of cloth or paper, which, instead of being a thing to hide, as is the canvas in most oil work, is normally allowed to contribute its own vital part to the final effect. Even when this ground is practically covered by the chalk, it still has its texture and its basic harmonizing tone to offer. Colored grounds, incidentally, can often save the artist half his customary effort, while improving his performance.

Value to the student

Pastel is particularly valuable to the art student, to whom this book is primarily addressed, for it is a medium for youth; for the impatient, the inquisitive, the impetuous, the exuberant, the adventurous. No other medium permits him with so little lost motion to investigate the mysteries of proportion, light and shade, color, texture, and composition. No other medium allows him greater freedom of individual expression. He can pitch right into his first subjects with little or no preliminary preparation; if they do not "arrive" they can easily be corrected or redone.

Some limitations

As against these and other merits, pastel has a few drawbacks—what medium has not? For example, an artist can all too easily smear his colors unpleasantly as he proceeds, or, through careless handling, he can later disfigure his finished results. His stick *will* break at an awkward moment; if he is caught in a sudden shower, rain may wash work away or spot it disastrously; fixative may deaden it; the most lovely colors may prove fugitive if exposed too long in bright light. In the past, some of the materials used in the manufacture of pastels were poisonous. Today, poisonous pigments are practically eliminated from the regular commercial product. Any finely ground powders, however, such as are in the composition of all pastels, can prove irritating to the throat and nose if continuously inhaled. After a morning's effort, the artist's nose and throat may be irritated by the dust.

But what are these few faults compared with all the virtues?

Roman Women *by Harvey Dinnerstein. Courtesy, Kenmore Galleries, Philadelphia. Giving the illusion of far more detail than is really there, the artist has blocked in his composition with broad, indistinct smudges of color, then defined edges and highlights with decisive light and dark strokes. The faces and the umbrella are virtually the only forms rendered with precise strokes, though even these are roughly painted on a rough surface.*

Brackman

2/Choosing Your Materials

Pastels are colored crayons, in some respects not unlike blackboard chalks, though more refined and available in a broader range of colors, as well as in various grades of hardness—soft, semi-hard, and hard. They are composed of colored pigment (organic or inorganic coloring matter), white color (clay, chalk, gypsum, zinc white, etc.), and a binding medium. These ingredients are first mixed and then fashioned into round or square sticks about the thickness of a lead pencil and about one third as long.

Some artists make their own pastels. This is not particularly difficult and it insures one the hues he wants. See Ralph Mayer's *The Artist's Handbook of Materials and Techniques* (Viking) for directions.

But most artists generally prefer to use one of the many commercial brands. These are made in four, seven, and sometimes eight, tones of each color, ranging from full chromatic strength to subtle tints. The lightest are usually the softest, dark ones being harder because they contain more colored pigment and less chalk.

Pastels

Soft pastels are more widely used than semi-soft or hard pastels because the soft variety will produce the broadest, most painterly effects. Semi-soft pastels produce somewhat crisper, more linear strokes, and are therefore useful for accents, detailed work, and linear definition. Hard pastels (which are often rectangular) are best for preliminary drawing and for an occasional precise stroke in the final stages of a painting, but their effect is far too linear for most painting purposes. Thus, many pastellists will lay in their composition and preliminary drawing with hard pastels, but are most likely to complete the painting with the soft variety, with occasional help from semi-soft pastels in the final stages.

These commercial crayons may be had in small or large sets, or in single sticks. Certain colors are more permanent than others. One will gradually learn to avoid the fugitive hues if he wishes his work to endure. The degree of permanency varies with different makes; it is indicated in the lists provided by some manufacturers of pastels.

Study in Pastel *by Robert Brackman. Courtesy, Grand Central Art Galleries, New York. The figure is built up with small strokes of heavily applied color, much like the artist's oil paintings. The drapery and chair are left unfinished to produce the casual effect known as a vignette. The artist relies on the texture of the paper to "blend" his strokes, and the rough surface is allowed to show through at many points to produce a lively effect. Aside from a few notes of shadow along the edges of the figure, the background is untouched.*

The beginner would do well to purchase a basic set of soft pastels, consisting of about 20 colors. To this nucleus, he can then gradually add until eventually he has an assortment ample to meet the most exacting demands. Here are some typical pastels of the Weber line; these, like most other makes, come in several degrees of hardness. By no means would all of them be needed for any single picture:

Black	**Browns**	**Greens**
White	Brown Red	Blue Green
Grays	Burnt Sienna	(Viridian Hue)
Black Gray	Burnt Umber	Chrome Green
Blue Gray	Raw Sienna	(Yellow Green)
Brown Gray	Raw Umber	Emerald Green
	VanDyke Brown	Terre Verte
	Deep Brown	Olive Green
Blues		Deep Green
Cerulean Blue Hue		
Cobalt Blue		
Prussian Blue	**Reds**	
Ultramarine	Crimson Madder	**Yellows**
	Flesh Ochre	Cadmium Yellow
Violets	Geranium	Chrome Yellow
Blue Violet	Light Red	Chrome Orange
Red Violet	Indian Red	Lemon Yellow
Mauve	Scarlet	Naples Yellow
Deep Violet	Vermilion	Yellow Ochre
Deep Purple	Cadmium Red	Golden Ochre

The firm of M. Grumbacher manufactures a satisfactory grade of pastels, and makes a half-hard crayon which is especially useful in portrait work, where detail is needed in the final stages.

Other crayons

Charcoal sticks and pencils can be useful in certain techniques for sketching in. The rectangular black, sanguine, and brown chalk crayons called Conté are completely reliable, and are sometimes used in combination with pastel for preliminary drawing and for linear accents.

Oil pastels are a new and popular product, with quite a different character from the traditional pastels discussed in this book. Because of their oil content, the colors are deeper and more luminous, with a corresponding lack in the subtlety and "bloom" that are unique to traditional pastels. It is best to use oil pastels by themselves—not in combination with other pastels. Although oil pastels are not dealt with in this volume, many traditional pastel techniques, described here, will apply to this new and promising medium.

Paper

Almost as important as the pastels themselves are the various surfaces or "grounds" on which they are used. These are of many kinds, permitting the pastellist a broad range of selection.

Paper is one of the most popular grounds. Its choice for each new piece of work is a vital matter, for although paper need not necessarily be expensive, it should always be appropriate to one's subject, technique, and mood. There are numerous types made in a wide range of colors and textures to suit every purse and purpose. For any serious effort—and especially if permanence is desired—only the highest quality should be considered. The best papers are manufactured from linen and cotton rags, and are sized to prevent the spreading of any applied color, such as liquid color, which may be used in conjunction with pastel. As to dimensions, many pastel papers measure approximately 19″ x 25″. There are also sheets 22″ x 28″, 20″ x 30″, 24″ x 34″, 26″ x 40″, and 30″ x 40″, varying according to make. If one wishes to work on still larger paper, rolls may be had about 60″ wide by 10 yards or so in length.

There can obviously be no hard and fast rule concerning one's choice. The beginner must gradually experiment with many kinds in order to find those which best suit his individual needs.

A certain roughness or *tooth* is essential. On a very smooth surface, the pastel fails to adhere properly, and it is difficult to superimpose one color over another. Inversely, too rough a paper should be avoided, as its surface will act as a file against the crayon, wasting the pastel, making the work difficult, and proving of no particular advantage. Papers heavily loaded with clay should be regarded with suspicion, as they are apt to stick together; they may also attract dampness which may subsequently cause mildew to develop. These unfortunate conditions can be controlled by the careful selection of paper and by the proper care of the finished picture.

Among the desirable papers are *Milano*, made in twelve colors, and *Toulon* in sixteen. The latter is of a fibrous type and softer than the former. These are distributed by Friedrichs, New York. Another paper is manufactured in fourteen tints by Grumbacher, also of New York. Hurlock and Weber of Philadelphia offer excellent lines of pastel boards. The superlative French papers of Canson & Montgolfier are available in art shops.

Colored grounds

Pastel is seldom used on a white ground (with the exception of white marble dust board and a few others), due to the fact that the colors appear darker when laid on, and seem to lack brilliance. On the other hand, a tinted paper, fairly low toned, provides a background very useful in qualifying the color placed upon it. It can play an especially important part in a drawing where a portion of the background can be left exposed. However, if white paper is preferred, or is the only one available, a wash of watercolor—either a pale, warm, grayish tone, or a soft tint of color—can be laid on. This can next be nearly sponged off, if one wishes, leaving a pleasant undertone. Such a tone washed paper should be dried carefully before use, as any moisture in the paper will alter the color of the pastels.

Two Nudes by Warren Brandt, 20" x 19¾". Collection, Mr. Joseph Richter. Courtesy, A. M. Sachs Gallery, New York. The artist applies his pastel in free, bold strokes which appear to have a life of their own, partially determined by the form, and partially independent of the form. Contours are then established by carefully placed lines which contain the lively color areas. Note where the artist uses a line to define the form and where he decides against using a line—which is equally important.

Pastel board and charcoal paper

Exceedingly useful as grounds are the fine sanded grain papers in blond color, and the pastel boards (paper mounted on board by the manufacturer) which come in many sizes and finishes, including marble dust and velvet, very like their names suggest.

Charcoal papers can be utilized if the *laid* texture is not too apparent. If it is, the up-and-down grain will show through the chalk as hollows and ridges, creating a rather stilted impression. Strathmore is an excellent American charcoal paper, comparable to the famous Ingres and Fabriano papers of Europe, also available here.

Parchment

The yellowish toned genuine parchment, or the substitute known as parchment paper, can be roughened a bit by rubbing lightly with fine emery paper. This creates the slight tooth necessary if pastel is to adhere. Either the genuine or the imitation parchment affords an easy working surface and imparts a soft velvety quality; its warm, golden tone makes a fine foil for the color used on it.

Mounting paper

While some artists dislike the pastel boards mentioned above (because they lack resilience), these boards possess one advantage. Being rigid, they offer far more resistance to injury than do papers. (The latter bend and buckle all too freely, thus loosening pigment particles.) The boards can also take washes of watercolor.

Similar advantages can be gained by mounting paper on a firm backing of cardboard, wallboard, etc. To do this mounting, the paper (before any drawing is done) is laid face down and covered completely on the back with drawing board paste or other suitable adhesive. Sometimes the paper is previously dampened with a brush or sponge. Then when the paper has expanded to its maximum size because of the dampness, the mounting board is laid onto it and rubbed down. The whole is next inverted (turned to normal position) and the paper rubbed on its face until smooth, usually with an extra paper under the hand to protect the surface. A roller or photographer's squeegee may be used in order to make certain that there are no air pockets between the paper and the mount, as the two must adhere throughout. The mounted paper is then allowed to dry beneath a weighted drawing board. In another method, the paper is first placed face down and dampened until it lies flat; then adhesive is applied along the four edges only, in a band an inch or so wide, after which the paper is inverted and pressed down to a suitable stiff mount. It will then dry flat if put beneath a weighted drawing board.

Paper can also be strained over a canvas stretcher, following the directions offered below for stretching canvas.

Pastel canvas

One of the most interesting grounds available to the pastel artist is canvas. Either cotton or linen makes up into a porous fabric on which a coating of pumice, silica, or other grainy pigment, mixed with paint, paste, or lacquer, is sprayed or thinly laid by the manufacturer. A dark or tinted ground is appropriate according to one's taste; tan, green, and gray tones are most frequently found.

These canvases can be purchased in sizes of about 42″ by 6 yards to a roll. M. Grumbacher manufactures both a velour pastel canvas and a sanded pastel canvas. Available through F. Weber are their own special canvases in various widths, as well as linen canvas prepared to order.

Stretching canvas

With your canvas selected, you may use it either unmounted or stretched. In the latter case, obtain from your dealer a frame or stretcher of proper size, preferably not over 24″ x 30″. You can assemble this easily, putting the patented strips together to form a rectangle, with all joints fitting smoothly. Next, cut your canvas 1½″ larger, in both dimensions, than the stretcher. Cover a sturdy table top with clean paper to avoid soiling the canvas while stretching, and place the canvas face down upon it. Lower the stretcher onto the canvas, making sure that the threads of the material run parallel to the two long sides, so as not to give the material a bias slant while stretching it. A light marking around the stretcher with a colored pencil to form guide marks may be helpful.

Starting at the center top, bend one edge of the canvas over the edge (side) of the stretcher frame and fasten it with a medium size tack. Repeat this process at the center of the bottom edge, pulling the canvas tight, and then proceed to the centers of the sides; the guide marks will help you to keep the material in line with the stretcher. Starting again at the top, place a row of tacks about 1½″ apart, working gradually to left and right of the center tack. Repeat on bottom and sides. The pull on the canvas should be even, to insure freedom from wrinkles.

At the corners, the excess fabric should be folded under smoothly and tacked down. Insert the stretcher keys (small triangular wedges of wood which come with the strips) and gently hammer these into the stretcher slots until the canvas surface becomes taut.

When paper is stretched on such a frame, less pulling is advisable than for canvas, and thumbtacks may be substituted for regular tacks.

Linen

Pastel can be used directly on medium weight natural linen, which affords a most agreeable silvery tone, particularly fine in effect. It should preferably be unsized; i.e., not filled with gelatine, glue, or other substance to stiffen it. If there is any question on this point, the linen should be washed in mild soap and water and dried. To make it ready for use, it should then be stretched over a wooden stretcher frame. Care should be taken in handling this type of ground, as it is sensitive to vibration.

Late Afternoon *by Aaron Shikler. Courtesy, Davis Galleries, New York. Although at first glance this painting seems to be rendered with great precision, it consists almost entirely of free, scrubby strokes; study the foliage in the background and at the model's feet, as well as the shadow side of her gown. Only the head is rendered with precision. The crisp, light edges of the gown are a few decisive, scribbly strokes, carefully placed.*

Three Dancers at their Toilette by Edgar Degas, 21½″ x 20½″. Courtesy, The Metropolitan Museum of Art, bequest of Mrs. H. O. Havemeyer, 1929. The H. O. Havemeyer Collection. In his mature pastels, Degas applied his color roughly and boldly, building up broad masses and minimizing detail. In this painting, the composition hinges on broad, relatively flat, roughly textured masses of dark and light.

Detail of Three Dancers at their Toilette *by Edgar Degas.*

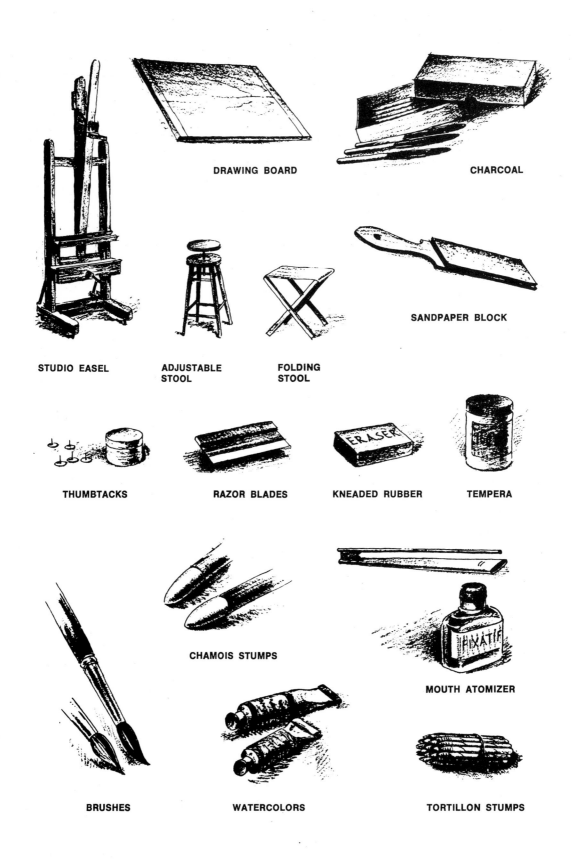

DRAWING BOARD

CHARCOAL

SANDPAPER BLOCK

STUDIO EASEL

ADJUSTABLE STOOL

FOLDING STOOL

THUMBTACKS

RAZOR BLADES

KNEADED RUBBER

TEMPERA

CHAMOIS STUMPS

MOUTH ATOMIZER

BRUSHES

WATERCOLORS

TORTILLON STUMPS

Here are some miscellaneous materials. Although for a time, at least, you can do without certain equipment such as an easel and an adjustable stool, do not handicap yourself through lack of essential materials and tools.

Additional materials

Here is a check list of some of the items of equipment essential to the beginner:

Easel and stool (many types are on the market)
Model stand (if portrait and figure work are to be done)
Drawing board (approximate size, 20″ x 27″, wood or thick fiber board)
Pastels (separate sticks or a set of assorted colors)
Work table for the pastels
A selection of toned papers and canvases
Sticks of charcoal (vine and hard types)
Thumbtacks
Kneaded rubber eraser
Razor blades or a sharp knife
Tortillons (rolled paper stumps) for blending
Chamois stumps for blending
Fixative and blower (hand or mouth type) or fixative in spray can ⎫ optional
Sandpaper block for sharpening charcoal
Artist's smock

The following can be included for variety in pastel technique, if needed:

Watercolors (including Chinese white), acrylic, tempera, casein,
or gouache paints
Carbon pencils
Brushes (watercolor types in red sable or oxhair)

Substituting chair for studio easel

In case you do not care to purchase a regular studio easel, an ordinary hard bottomed chair is a good substitute. Place the drawing board on the seat of the chair and prop it almost vertically against the chair back. A weight, such as a heavy book or a brick, should be put in front of the board to prevent it from slipping. Inasmuch as you have to sit while working at this improvised easel (as it is obviously not high enough to use if you are standing), a second chair can serve as a drawing stool. This arrangement works out very well indeed, though it makes it almost too easy for the student to forget that it is advisable for him to stand back occasionally and observe his work from a distance in order to check its proportions, values, color, and composition.

Work table

As to a work table for the pastels, any sturdy table will do, so long as it is not too large—you may want to swing it between yourself and the easel while working. My own work table is a reconstructed candlestand. The base has three legs (very convenient for fitting over the footboard of the easel) and a top measuring 20″ x 28″, provided with a raised rim, about an inch high, to prevent the pastels from rolling off. It also contains a small drawer, but this is not important. The height of the table should be considered with care—it might be adjustable—as it should always be at an easy working level whether you are sitting or standing. (Incidentally, in addition to my major work table, I have several others around the studio in case I need them to hold more pastels.)

Over this table I spread my pastels, the colors unsorted because this is the way in which I like to work, the scattering of the many colors proving a stimulus as I paint. It may take me a little longer to find the crayon I particularly want, but at the same time there is a subconscious selective judging of the whole mass of color on the table. From this scattered mass, forever changing, one color against another, the creative mind receives new impetus and ideas. (Those who wish to keep their pastels in orderly little boxes of separate colors may do so of course. They will no doubt stay clean longer.)

Taking stock

Once in every three or four months I clean and check my pastels, discarding the too short ones, replacing them with new ones which I keep on hand in half dozen lots. The soiled ones I wipe carefully with cleansing tissue. While doing all this, I wear a gauze mask (hospital type) to protect my nose and throat from the pastel dust. Most pastels today are free from poisonous substances, but a large amount cf the dust can be irritating.

Cathy *by Burton Silverman, 15" x 21½". Collection, Mr. & Mrs. Sol Sardinsky. Courtesy, Kenmore Galleries, Philadelphia. In rendering the complex forms of the human figure, one of the most valuable features of pastel is the ease with which the artist can build up a pattern of strokes that travel around the form to reveal three-dimensional contours. Notice the intricate play of curving strokes on the cylindrical arms and legs of the figure, and the contrasting vertical strokes which provide a counterpoint to the strokes on the figure.*

Study for The Long Black Veil *by Burton Silverman. Courtesy, Kenmore Galleries, Philadelphia. Pastel is especially suitable for capturing complex light effects with great speed. Here, the artist has rapidly stroked in the jagged shadow areas and the sparse notes of strong light on the faces, hands, and guitar. A broad, slashing stroke is used, and one has the impression that the artist worked rapidly to catch the fleeting light effect, which is likely to change so quickly. It is often worthwhile to decide whether detail will be concentrated in the light areas or in the shadow areas. In this painting, light defines detail, and shadow obscures it.*

3/Learning to Use Pastel

With equipment at hand, your inclination will be to get at your first subject immediately. Do this if you wish. Faster progress will probably be made in the end, however, if you just play around for two or three hours, trying your different crayons on a variety of grounds. This and the next few chapters are designed to aid you during this brief but important period.

Preparing your paper

For your very first experiments, scraps of paper should be adequate, though you may prefer to prepare your paper just as you would for a serious painting. In case you do, select any paper which strikes your fancy—preferably toned—and place two sheets on your drawing board, one superimposed on the other. Thumbtack them to the board, spacing the tacks about three inches apart all around. As you do this, smooth the paper gently from the center outward, getting the surface as firm and even as possible. Don't permit your fingernails to mar the paper, leaving unsightly shiny streaks which, in important work, might later prove unpleasant to work over. Such streaks might even detract from the ultimate result, particularly if sections of the paper are allowed to remain blank or only partly covered with pastel.

The object of using the paper double is to create a more resilient surface for the pastel to go into, and cling to, than a single sheet affords. This employment of double paper is especially helpful when combining charcoal with pastel; the charcoal glides along and there is less danger of breaking it—and your crayons, too—as you proceed.

Remedying buckling

As paper is hygroscopic (it absorbs moisture), a slight bulging of your double sheets may form overnight, especially if the atmosphere is abnormally damp. This bulging can usually be remedied by placing the board with the paper on it near a radiator or stove for a few minutes. If buckling still exists after this treatment, lift and replace the thumbtacks one at a time, meanwhile smoothing the paper near the outside edges with the fingers or the side of the hand, being very careful not to smudge the pastel in the process. A slight pulling at the edges of the paper, as each pin is removed and replaced, will generally overcome any excess wrinkling.

Preliminary procedure

With the paper in place on the drawing board, adjust the easel to a comfortable working height. Then secure the drawing board firmly by means of the top sliding clamp on the easel; this will prevent the board from falling off if the easel is shifted as the work progresses. Also, you may wish to adjust the easel to a forward angle, with the top of the board nearer to you than the bottom. This is often more comfortable than having the board vertical, and it permits any excess pastel dust to fall to the floor instead of sliding down and adhering to the lower parts of the picture.

Fine line practice

You should now experiment to see what sort of a linear tool your pastel is—what kinds of line you can draw with it, naturally and easily. Try some reasonably straight strokes—horizontal, vertical, slanting. Try also some strokes which are back and forth, up and down, and diagonal. Now make some curves, loops, or round and round strokes; spirals are good. Wandering strokes might be followed by experiments with dabs and dots—stipple, as this technique is called when an area is very finely dotted.

This does not mean that you are to copy slavishly the examples illustrated in the book. Not at all. Your only purpose is to get acquainted, in the most natural way, with the characteristics of your crayon as a linear tool, so experiment with anything that occurs to you. Vary the crayons, selecting some soft, some medium, some hard. Vary your pressure, also, to learn just how each crayon will *take* under different pressures—this will of course depend somewhat on your paper—and to discover under what conditions your point will crumble or break. Vary your way of holding the crayon; and, last but not least, vary the speed with which you make your strokes, drawing some slowly and deliberately, and some with extreme dash and vigor.

Speaking of "the most natural way" of conducting your work, that phrase should always be kept uppermost in your mind, not only in conjunction with these exercises, but in your subsequent work as well. True art can result only from using one's materials with full regard for all their properties, both good and bad. Stated conversely, *it is never true art to force a medium to do that which it is not naturally fitted to do.*

Broad stroke practice

For certain purposes, and especially when you wish to cover large areas of the paper quickly, the side of the crayon can be employed much more effectively than the point. To demonstrate this, hold a pastel stick on its side—often a broken piece will do—and apply strokes to your ground in all sorts of experimental ways. You will find that by varying your pressure and by utilizing a diversity of natural movements of your arm, wrist, and fingers in various directions, certain definite types of stroke will come almost automatically to your hand, some of them quite different in character from those produced with the point of the tool.

Do not attempt to imitate in detail the strokes shown in the book; they are intended only to give you some idea of the proper approach. The thing that counts is to discover what your own pastels are capable of accomplishing on your own papers.

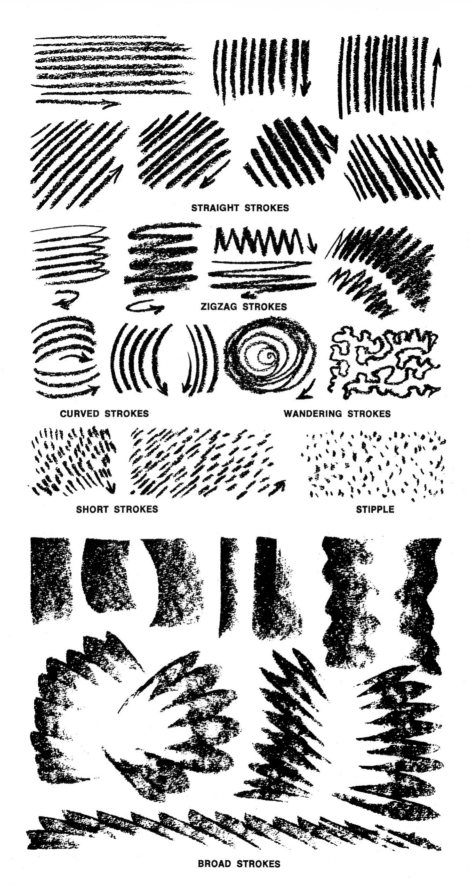

STRAIGHT STROKES

ZIGZAG STROKES

CURVED STROKES

WANDERING STROKES

SHORT STROKES

STIPPLE

BROAD STROKES

Try many such strokes with soft, semi-soft, and hard pastels to learn about the medium before you try your first painting.

Direct tone building: mass shading

It is but a step from this practice in making fine and broad strokes to building areas of tone, differing both in technical quality and in degree of light and dark. Most of the examples shown consist merely of lines touching or overlapping to cover a large part of the paper area. They were not smoothed with the finger or stump. Crosshatching is a type of work in which lines drawn in one direction are crossed by those in another; a great variety of crosshatching is possible. In all the examples shown, the strokes are quite conspicuous. Some areas of pastel tone are made practically solid, showing little evidence of the component strokes; work of this sort is often called mass shading.

Most of the examples illustrated were drawn with a rather hard crayon, quite sharply pointed. Obviously you cannot expect such effects from softer crayons unless you work in large scale. As a matter of fact, much of your practicing should preferably be done in large size and quite boldly. Do not be timid!

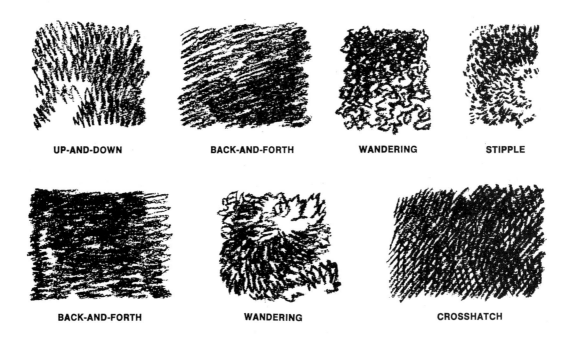

UP-AND-DOWN   BACK-AND-FORTH   WANDERING   STIPPLE

BACK-AND-FORTH   WANDERING   CROSSHATCH

Experiment with strokes in various directions to produce a wide range of movements and textures.

Manipulated tone

Line work or tone work may be purposely rubbed or *smooched* until quite smooth, using the thumb, finger, a piece of chamois, or a *stump* of chamois or paper. Sometimes in such cases the lines are still quite plainly to be seen. Again they are entirely obliterated. Still again, a tone is first rubbed smooth and then is later gone over, in whole or part, with additional lines or tones. Tone areas may be either ungraded (flat) or graded (graduated). You will want to try out all of these hints.

(Though we are postponing color considerations until the next chapter, these exercises may use color or black and white.)

In this work, it is best to stand at an easel, gaining the ability to work with the paper in an upright position. For careful passages, some artists like to use a painter's mahlstick as a rest for the hand or wrist, but the greater control you can acquire without such aid the better.

If you are left handed, many of your strokes will quite naturally be opposite in direction to those of the right handed person, so take this into account in performing these exercises.

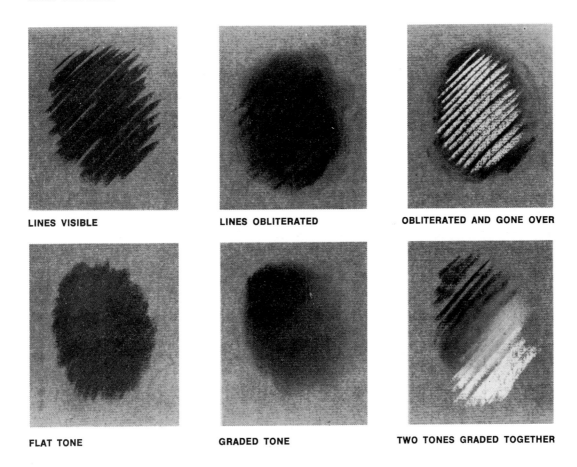

LINES VISIBLE   LINES OBLITERATED   OBLITERATED AND GONE OVER

FLAT TONE   GRADED TONE   TWO TONES GRADED TOGETHER

Try producing tone simply with lines—then manipulate the lines in various ways to develop other kinds of tone and texture.

Influence of paper

The next examples of strokes on various surfaces demonstrate more clearly than words what a striking influence paper surface exerts on pastel tone. These specimen areas were done with *one* crayon which was used on different papers. The variation in appearance resulted almost wholly from the diversified textures of the papers. The tone at the top was in each case left unsmooched; the one below was rubbed with the finger. Experiment for yourself in this direction, trying a variety of papers in various textures, handmade and machine made.

FINE GRAINED CHARCOAL PAPER	**COARSER GRAINED CHARCOAL PAPER**	**HANDMADE DRAWING PAPER**
MACHINE MADE DRAWING PAPER	**ROUGH HANDMADE WATERCOLOR PAPER**	**COLD PRESSED HANDMADE WATERCOLOR PAPER**

The texture of your paper has a distinct effect on your strokes. Try many surfaces to find your favorites.

The author's method

I hope I have made clear that it is not my aim to tell you dogmatically exactly how you *must* apply pastel to your ground, but rather to guide you in discovering the methods which seem natural to you. Each artist gradually develops his own pet methods. Here, for example, is the one which I have come to prefer for my own work. It is a popular method with many others, too, and well worth a thorough trial on your part during this experimental period.

Take a good sized sheet of paper and place it on the board and easel. Holding a crayon firmly between thumb and forefinger (slightly closing the little finger and using the back and tip of it as a pivot and brace), swing the whole hand about in a free arc. Through this practice you will soon develop complete control over the direction of the crayon. This method I use both for building an even tone on the paper—by exerting a uniform pressure continuously with the crayon—and for grading tone from dark to light, or from light to dark, by gradually diminishing or increasing the pressure.

Using much the same procedure, you should next experiment with straight sweeping lines, letting the hand go free from the board and controlling the pressure of the crayon with the action of the whole arm instead of with the little finger.

Cleanliness

One of your main jobs in doing pastel work is to learn to keep your paper clean. In applying pastel (in portraiture particularly, where a crisp technique is desired, with as few erasures as possible), it is usually the best procedure to work from the top of the paper downward and from the left side to the right (if you are right handed), in order to leave a clear space on the lower right hand surface to support the drawing hand, if and when it becomes necessary to place it there while painting. This uncovered section can be filled in at the completion of the work. Thus, smudging will be kept at an absolute minimum.

Corrections

The less correcting one does to pastel work the better. If it becomes necessary to undertake any drastic changes or erasures as the picture develops, the edge of a razor blade can be employed lightly to scrape off the pastel where the changes are to be made. Kneaded rubber is also useful; while this is sometimes employed for rubbing, careless or vigorous rubbing may injure the fibers of the paper, so more often the kneaded eraser is utilized as an instrument for *lifting* pigment particles from the surface. In order to accomplish this, the rubber is pressed firmly, but evenly, against the offending area; the pigment particles adhere to it and are thus lifted away. This erased section can then be redrawn to harmonize with the rest of the picture. (It is well to keep the eraser clean by wiping it frequently on a cloth or tissue or by rubbing it on scrap paper; otherwise it may drive unwanted color back into the paper.)

When erasures are required on grainy surfaces—notably on marble dust board where it would be difficult for a regular eraser to penetrate—a clean rag can be dampened with a small quantity of fixative and lightly passed over the surface. This operation can be repeated, if necessary, until the area is sufficiently clean. Remember to press lightly to avoid damaging the surface.

Using unmounted canvas

All through this chapter we have spoken of paper. When you have gained a reasonable degree of familiarity with paper, you should cut from your roll a piece of pastel canvas of the size wanted. Place this on the drawing board and pin it down with thumbtacks all the way around (unless, of course, you wish to stretch it as described earlier). It is not necessary to do much stretching, as canvas has a natural tendency to lie flat. No cushioning is required as this material is thick enough to use alone. Now try on this canvas some of the experiments described for paper.

Linear and tonal approaches

I might point out, as an aid to the beginner, that there are two basic approaches to blocking in or constructing one's selected subject.

The first and most common of these is the linear or outline approach—drawing outlines of the larger forms and the leading subdivisions. It seems almost instinctive with youngsters to outline everything that they draw. When they first attempt to draw the front view of a face, for instance, they usually start with a circle—the approximate outline of the face—and, for the body, draw another more or less circular outline, and so on. Even when they start to use tone or color, they still rely to a considerable extent on outlines of the basic forms and of their component parts.

A majority of teachers of drawing, taking advantage of this natural tendency, encourage even their more advanced students to draw in this same way, first outlining their forms, later using these outlines as a guide for the tone and color, whether or not the outlines are allowed to remain in the final work. This method works well and can be recommended.

The alternate approach is to depict forms more as we see them in nature, not surrounded by outlines, but as masses or shapes of tone or color. To exemplify this, if we examine an apple, we actually see no outline around it, so if we represent it in outline we are using a man made convention. If we draw or paint the apple directly in tone or color, however, as the more or less circular mass which we see, we are in a sense being more logical than when we outline it.

Very often these two approaches are combined. The artist sketches part of his subject in outline, and tentatively indicates a bit of tone or color. When this preliminary experimenting has produced a reasonably satisfying result, he then proceeds with his final rendering.

Form and color

The terms *form* and *color* really interlock, for in the painter's language each is definitely a part of the other. Form may be said to be the shape and structure of anything, and the power to represent form through various values and hues of color is the basis of all good painting. This ability, developed by constant practice and study, should become second nature to the artist.

A student may begin by asking, "But just how do I go about *seeing* form, and how do I use color to *express* it?" This can best be answered by reference to a specific example. Let us suppose the student is facing an earthen jug set on a table against a background of drapery. Let him first ask of himself, "What shape is this jug?" Next, "What degrees of lightness or of darkness have its various parts in relation to the table beneath it and the background behind it? How does its light side compare with its dark? What of its hues?" Through such self-interrogation, he gradually learns to observe, judge, and paint such things correctly, recognizing at last the truth of the statement that one can get structure and shape into a picture by expressing form through color.

Color is perhaps the most stimulating element of painting, but unless it is founded on good construction of form, it can be but a superficial thing. A sense of color is principally an instinctive feeling—a perception with which some are naturally more richly endowed than others. This need not be too discouraging to the beginner, for many painters who do not possess a fine sense of color have other admirable talents or skills necessary in painting. Even if their restricted ability to handle color limits them to the use of less daring combinations than others, they may nevertheless achieve very successful pictures. Later, their color sense will gradually develop.

The Bath *by Burton Silverman. Courtesy, Kenmore Galleries, Philadelphia. Following in the tradition of Degas, this contemporary artist studies a bather in an intimate, unselfconscious pose. Note the rough texture of his strokes, which seem deceptively random. Actually, the free strokes follow the form of the body, and even the diagonal strokes of the shadow are carefully directed to place this dark patch firmly on the wall. The deep shadow behind the model enhances the feeling of deep space.*

After the Bath *by Edgar Degas. Courtesy, The Metropolitan Museum of Art, bequest of Mrs. H. O. Havemeyer, 1929. The H. O. Havemeyer Collection. Because pastel has many of the qualities of a drawing medium—including great speed of execution—it is particularly suitable for the rapid rendering of informal action poses. Here, the greatest of all pastellists catches his model in an intimate, momentary pose. The strokes are applied freely on rough paper, enhancing the casual mood.*

4 / Color Manipulation

Until now, we have said almost nothing about color, for it has mattered little whether most of the suggested experiments were carried out in color or in black and white. In much pastel work, however, color is obviously a main concern, so it is now time for you to learn something of rudiments such as color mixing or blending.

We have described pastel work as *direct*, and this is true. When making a pastel, practically the entire job (excepting the thinking!) is done upon the final paper, with the crayons employed exactly as they come from the manufacturer's box. Pastels, in other words, are not blended by the artist upon a palette before application, as are oil paints, or mixed together with water, as are watercolors, but they are blended or mixed directly upon the painting ground itself—the paper or canvas—during, or immediately following, their application.

In normal use, pastels differ from most other media—for example, relatively transparent oil or tempera paints—in that they possess only surface light, and in appearance closely resemble the effect of dry, opaque pigment. Therefore the pastellist, unlike the painter in oils, is not concerned about the choice of the right painting medium and correct brushes, nor does he worry about glazes and the time allowance for drying out of the painting. We have already seen that he has merely his sticks of chalk and a piece of paper, canvas, pasteboard, or other suitable ground with which to record his impressions—tools which make possible the most direct and simple method of painting known to man, the pure color being applied exactly as it is without the addition of a liquid vehicle or medium. Given a good paper or canvas, and good pastels—and, of course, the know-how—work of unusual quality and permanence can be achieved. This work will not discolor or crack as paintings in oil may, but as we have said before, it must be protected, or it will smear or powder off the paper.

Application of pastels

Pastel can be applied by a number of normal or legitimate means, which fall roughly into four classes.

1. The artist can draw in line, much as he would with charcoal or soft pencil.

2. The artist can work wholly in tone by covering the entire surface of his paper with color by means of the blunted ends of his crayons, or by using them sidewise, losing the impression of line for one of mass. In such work, the color of the background upon which he draws—his paper or canvas—is relatively unimportant.

3. He can follow a middle course, employing the sharpened point of the pastel crayon in a stroking or drawing method to form somewhat broken tone on his ground—a tinted ground is generally preferred—often allowing the tone of the paper to play its part in the general scheme, as it will not be covered everywhere with pastel.

4. The pastels can be blended or smoothed together, either in the whole work or in parts, with tortillon stumps (of paper), chamois stumps, or the fingers.

Methods of color mixing

There are a number of techniques of mixing colors in pastel work. Any one of the following basic methods is acceptable; any or all of them may be combined according to the creative aim and skill of the artist. While each student will gradually develop his own technical preferences, he should, for a time, endeavor to avoid the all too common habit of using only one set method. To do so might easily make the means become more important in his mind than the end, and his pictorial results might therefore appear mannered, with the technical method forcing itself unpleasantly upon the spectator's attention. Instead, the artist should gradually so master all those methods of application which are natural to his medium that he can later draw on them at will, subconsciously turning to that method, or combination of methods, which will best serve his purpose.

Blending by superposition: stroking method

In this technique, the different colors to be mixed are stroked together as they are applied, one color laid over or into another by exerting fairly even pressure on the crayons. There is no smoothing or blending of the color except that which is done with the crayons themselves. The ability thus to lay or build a tone is of decided value—especially for figure or portrait work, where exact modeling of shapes is frequently necessary. In this stroking method, a certain desirable length of crayon is necessary—not less than $1\frac{1}{2}''$ to $2''$—for an easy *swinging* motion of the hand and to maintain a feeling of balance of the crayon as it is held. The pastellist must at the same time be able to see the working end of the crayon traveling over the ground, so too short a crayon should be discarded without regret.

Blending by crosshatching

In a variation of the direct stroking method, one color is first stroked onto the paper —usually all the strokes taking the same general direction—and then a second color is added but with the strokes crossing the first at an angle. Sometimes several colors are thus employed. By this means, the colors automatically mingle; the effect is often extremely pleasing.

Blending by juxtaposition

In a third method of color blending, the eye becomes a blending agent. Tiny dots or dabs of different colors are juxtaposed or interlaced with a minimum of actual blending.

Stroke different colors one over the other in the same direction, without blending.

Stroke different colors one over the other in opposing directions, without blending. This is crosshatching.

Try crosshatching at a different angle.

Apply tiny dots or dabs of different colors, without blending. The colors blend in the viewer's eye. This is called stippling or pointillism.

Enliven a dull or overworked passage by feathering with a hard crayon.

Blend strokes together with the fingers or a stump. But do not overdo it!

The eye automatically merges the different hues, especially as the spectator stands back from the work. Thus is created that vibrant, lively effect described as *broken color*. The method is sometimes known as *divisionism* or *pointillism*. The ground, particularly when tinted, customarily plays a definite part in this technique, as it is almost impossible, and usually undesirable, to cover it entirely with the pastel. This use of juxtaposed color can scarcely be improved upon for certain purposes, notably in landscape or flower painting. This should be viewed from a distance of several feet.

Feathering

Some of these so-called normal methods of applying pastel might, in certain applications, also be termed "curative" methods, as they can be utilized in improving work which has developed faults. For instance, in producing a pastel, it occasionally happens that a particular part gradually becomes dull or lifeless in tone, the intrinsic charm of the medium perhaps being spoiled by excessive rubbing in. Again, large areas of solid color may prove to be monotonous.

These faults may often be remedied by what is known as *feathering*—one of the most valuable aids in pastel work, for it makes possible the substitution of vitality for lifelessness, and the breaking up of uninteresting surfaces to give a fresher, more spontaneous appearance.

To do this feathering, take a hard crayon, hold it firmly with the thumb and forefinger, and, using my method of rocking the hand on the little finger, *feather* the color by stroking with an upward and downward movement over the surface where the fresher appearance is needed. (The effect accomplished through feathering resembles somewhat the barbs of a quill—hence the name.) No one color is selected for this work; it depends entirely on the general tone of these bad areas as to just what colors should be introduced into them to improve them.

A little practice will enable the student to make feathering a valuable assistant in many phases of his pastel work. Lights and shadows, for example, can be feathered together, and hard edges softened.

Blending by rubbing

Last but not least—in fact it often comes first in point of use—we have the blending of pastels through rubbing or smooching with the fingers, thumb, tortillons, or chamois stump. This kind of blending can give a rich bloom to the colors—an admirable quality —but if the rubbing is overdone, the color tends to dull, and the picture may appear fuzzy and weak in tone. Used with discrimination and taste, this method has the great advantage of bringing the tones together quickly, so the work may proceed rapidly.

Often all of these methods are combined in a single painting.

Blending complementary or analagous colors

When blending colors, particularly by the rubbing method just described, the beginner is occasionally puzzled to notice that when certain brilliant hues are rubbed together the resultant hue is dull and dead—perhaps gray or brown—while other equally bright hues when similarly blended create brilliant results.

The explanation is simple. Briefly, colors which in pigment form are opposites or complements grow dull in admixture. Green and red, for instance, are such opposites, being wholly unrelated hues having no common family resemblance; therefore they tend to annihilate each other in mixture, producing a dull grayish, greenish, or brownish effect. Similarly, orange and blue neutralize each other in mixture, as do yellow and violet.

Pairs of analogous (related) hues, on the contrary—especially if intense—create, in admixture, other hues of similar intensity. Bright red and bright yellow, for example, give us, when mixed, a third bright color, orange. Yellow and blue give green, and red and blue give violet. (We are talking here only of pigment colors, as used in pastels— not of spectrum colors as dealt with by the physicist, for the colors of the spectrum, of which light is composed, follow quite different laws.)

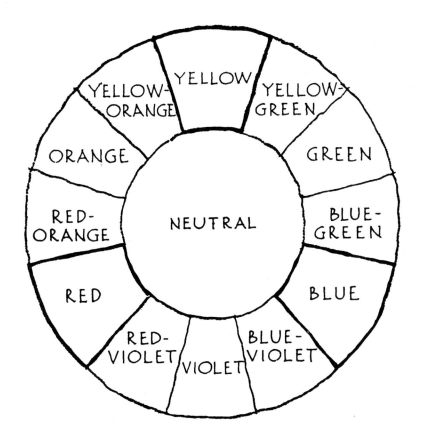

Pigment colors which are opposite on the color wheel (complements), such as red and green, blue and orange, yellow and violet, tend to neutralize each other in mixture. For example, if you wish to dull a red tone, work green into it. If many colors are mixed together, they produce a neutral tone. If complementary colors are used in reasonably large areas, side by side, each tends to intensify the other. For instance, if you wish to make an orange area seem brighter, use blue or blue-violet in adjacent or surrounding areas. Paradoxically, an opposite effect results when areas are extremely small.

Juxtaposition of complements

One of the oddest things about color is that the complementary hues which tend to neutralize each other in mixture—colors such as red and green, which, as we have just seen, create dull grayish or brownish hues when blended—have just the opposite effect when placed side by side. If, for example, a fair sized area of green is placed next to a similar area of red, each will actually appear to intensify the other through contrast. This is true, also, of yellow and violet.

The pastellist often takes advantage of this intensifying quality of complementary colors. To illustrate, if he wishes to make a yellow or orange building appear very bright and sunny, he may purposely use the opposite color—blue or violet—in adjoining areas such as shadows or sky.

Influence of color area

The smaller these contrasting areas are, the less will this principle apply. We have already seen that when tiny areas of opposite colors are placed side by side they are optically merged so that they annihilate one another, producing a somewhat neutral effect. As proof of this, if you cover a paper with hundreds of closely spaced dots of all sorts of hues, and then stand at some distance from it, your eye will gain the impression of a vibrant tone of neutral hue.

Some artists, unfamiliar with the change in effect of colors according to their area, do pastel paintings using relatively bright colors in small areas only, and then wonder why their finished work looks dead. To avoid dull looking results, one must keep in mind the rule that *color areas, to count to full advantage, must not be too small*. This is especially true if such areas are to be further reduced through reproduction (as in books or magazines), or viewed from a considerable distance.

Student practice

You will doubtless want to try for yourself experiments such as I have just described, using colored crayons of soft, medium, and hard varieties. You will find that some of the crayons will be more sympathetic than others to your own way of working. Furthermore, you may be alarmed at the tendency of many of the crayons to break if you bear down too heavily. But by practicing the method of holding the crayons, which has already been described, this annoyance can be mitigated to a great degree; one must expect a certain amount of breakage as the work goes along.

During this practice, particular attention should be given to observing and memorizing the way in which various hues affect one another, both in mixture and in juxtaposition.

Pastel painting vs. pastel drawing

In talking about technique, the question is often asked, "What is a pastel painting, and why is it different from a pastel drawing?" We have seen that as one performs experiments like those so far described, he utilizes various methods and so, quite naturally, creates a diversity of effects. A few of these effects seem like drawings; more of them are really paintings. When we speak of a *pastel painting*, we customarily assume that the whole, or practically the whole surface of the paper or canvas is covered with pastel, the effect actually being quite like that of an oil painting (that is, a solid feeling prevails). The opposite is true in a *pastel drawing*, where the economical use of pastel, usually in a linear manner, is the dominant factor in producing a suggestion, rather than the full tonal development, of the subject. The terms are employed by most artists very loosely, however, and a successful combination of the two techniques is often seen.

Woman Bathing *by Edgar Degas. Courtesy, The Metropolitan Museum of Art, bequest of Mrs. H. O. Havemeyer, 1929. The H. O. Havemeyer Collection. Degas relied on the texture of his paper to break up his strokes into lively, broken color. Boldly applied to rough paper, his strokes retain soft edges, and contours are sharpened only occasionally by a dark line, with most of the painting remaining out of focus.*

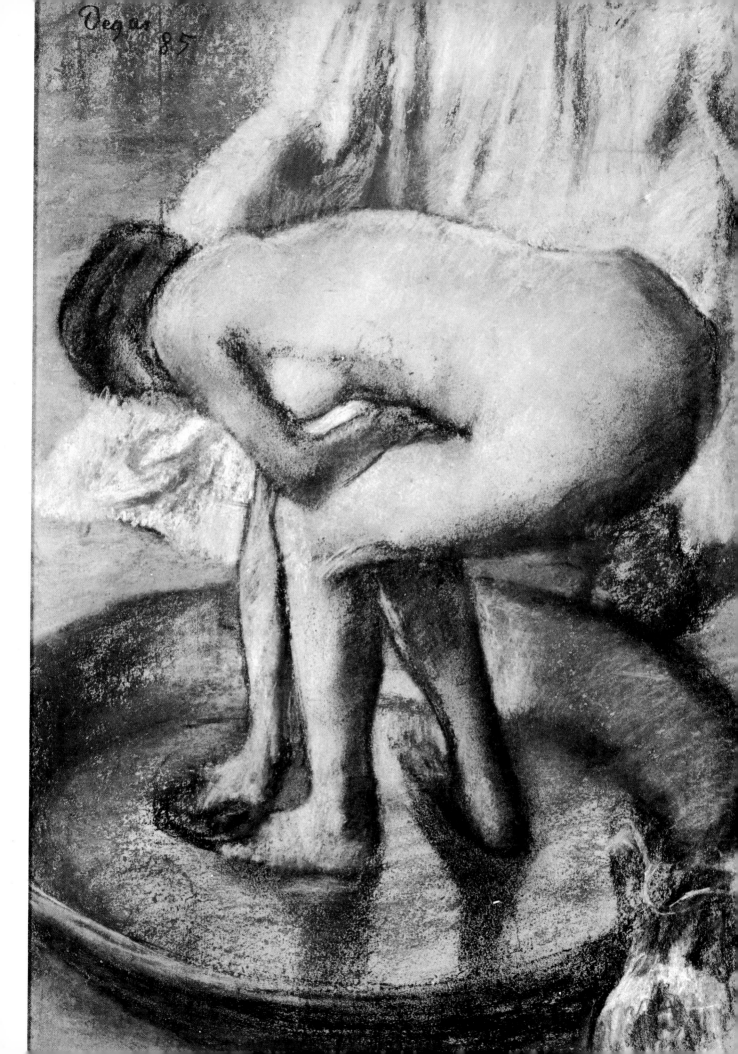

5/Pastel Combined
With Other Media

Some pastellists are purists; they strenuously object to the use of any other media in combination with pastel. But what can be the harm in combining two or more media which possess a natural affinity, so long as the final results have esthetic quality? Many of our most successful pastellists have freely combined their pastels with any media which have proven amenable, among them charcoal and various types of watercolors, gouaches, and acrylics. Degas combined pastel with a monotype underpainting and often added gouache.

Charcoal, for instance, is employed much like the pastel itself. Pen and ink, or brush and ink, are occasionally utilized, generally for doing vigorous underdrawing or underpainting which is partly or wholly hidden by subsequent pastel applications. I recall some very effective sketches in which a crisp delineation in brown ink was superimposed with thin applications of pastel, rubbed in sufficiently to permit the ink to show through, though in a veiled manner.

The most useful of all the supplementary media, so far as my own experience is concerned, are the various watercolors, whether transparent or opaque.

Transparent watercolors

The use of regular watercolors—those sometimes designated as *transparent* in contrast with the more opaque or *body* types—appears to be largely limited to the tinting of paper to a suitable color to serve as a ground for the pastel, especially when colored paper of desirable hue is not at hand. Normally, the paper is uniformly tinted by freely and quickly flowing a wash of the watercolor, greatly diluted with water, over the entire surface with the aid of a large brush. With experience, one acquires the knack of distributing the paint so uniformly that the paper, when dry, bears an even tint.

Now and then, the artist sketches his subject first, perhaps in pencil, next tinting different areas with a variety of appropriate watercolor hues. In either case, once the watercolor is dry, the pastel is applied just as it would be on any colored paper, some

---

Mlle. Valtesse de la Bigne *by Edouard Manet, 21¾" x 14". Courtesy, The Metropolitan Museum of Art, bequest of Mrs. H. O. Havemeyer, 1929. The H. O. Havemeyer Collection. Working on canvas, whose texture shows distinctly in the dress and the hair, Manet applied his pastel with a combination of soft, almost brush-like strokes, for the hair; delicate, indistinct strokes for the face; crisp strokes for the collar; and broad, flat strokes for the dress.*

areas of the paper being completely hidden, perhaps, while others are allowed to show through in spots to modify the final result.

Various watercolor pigments affect the paper differently from a textural standpoint, some of them creating a *tooth* which takes the pastel most sympathetically. Only by experimenting will you acquaint yourself with such possibilities.

Opaque watercolors: gouache, tempera, acrylic

Still more useful—at least this has been my experience—are watercolors of the class commonly referred to as *opaque* or *body* colors. Basically, these are practically the same as transparent watercolors excepting that they have been made opaque by the addition of heavy white pigments, so that they have considerable substance or body.

Like transparent watercolors, opaque colors are mainly used by the pastellist for preparing grounds of suitable hue and texture for the subsequent superposition of pastel. Colored body washes are particularly good as a basis for pastel landscapes, producing sprightly tones of great charm. Better results are generally to be had on toned grounds rather than on white.

The three best known types of opaque or body colors are gouache, tempera, and acrylic. The main difference among these three lies in their mixing medium, gouache being soluble in water, even after it has been applied, while tempera and acrylic dry to a more nearly insoluble state. Various makes of colors are on sale under these names; they differ considerably, one from another.

In the selection of tempera and acrylic paints for use in conjunction with pastel, especial care should be taken, for if too much medium has been employed in their manufacture, they will dry to a hard, enamel-like surface unsuitable for the subsequent application of pastel crayons. Therefore the making of a few trial tests with different types of tempera and acrylic colors might prove advisable. For such tests, dilute the paint with water to a thin wash; apply it to trial papers until the right consistency is found; dry them and then stroke the pastel crayon over them. The paint should dry to a matte finish and the pastel should take on it sympathetically and cling to it with ease.

The various kinds of gouache also vary to such a degree that similar tests might prove sound insurance. Occasionally the artist makes his own gouache paints through grinding and mixing, but unless he intends to use a very large amount of paint, there is little point in doing this.

In addition to the types of gouache commonly carried by dealers, there are prepared paints available which closely resemble gouache and do very well as a substitute. Among them are Winsor & Newton designers' colors, which are put up in tube form in a wide choice of hues. I have listed seven of these colors for mixing washes—an ample number for the student at the start. All of them are permanent with the exception of sky blue, which has a rating of being moderately fast to light.

| Permanent White | Cadmium Red | Alizarin Crimson | Sky Blue |
| Ivory Black | Cadmium Yellow | Burnt Umber | |

Chinese white watercolor (zinc oxide), which can be purchased in either jars or tubes, makes a fine gouache-like body wash when mixed with ordinary watercolor paints. Use only the best grade watercolors to insure a smooth texture of paint, as the cheaper grades are apt to be grainy, due to their inferior manufacture. A little extra expense for good colors is well repaid in the pleasure of working with them.

The use of body washes

Whatever the type of body color selected, the first step in its use is the preparation of the paper. Take a small and not too coarse sponge, wring it out in clear water, and pass it lightly over the surface of your pastel paper. Turn the paper over and repeat the process, and then turn it back again for a third and final sponging. The paper should now be damp, but not wet. Stretch it on the drawing board, fastening it in place with thumbtacks all around, or with dampened gummed tape, which should overlap the paper edges by at least one half inch in order to withstand the tension as the paper dries. When the paper has dried out taut (which requires only a short time), it is ready for sketching in the picture. This is accomplished with a carbon pencil. The lines should be fairly strong so that they will later show through the semi-opaque wash; thus a delicate veil of color will soften the lines, giving them a grayish quality which can be of great advantage later in the pastel work.

With the sketching completed, if you have decided on one color only for the wash, mix enough of this color at a time (in a saucer or similar vessel) to cover the whole surface, for nothing is more annoying than to have to stop work for lack of sufficient paint and begin all over again to mix. Use either a bristle brush (No. 6 would be about the right size) or, if you prefer, a red sable or oxhair watercolor brush, and start across the top of the paper, working quickly across and then proceeding downward, brushing the color onto the paper. With practice, you will soon acquire the knack. If you decide to use several tones of wash, they can be mixed in the compartments of the watercolor box, or in a nest of saucers. Then, when applied, they can gradually be merged one into another, or, if it better serves your purpose, each distinct area can be colored and allowed to dry, after which the next can be done with another color, and so on. The important thing is not to get the washes too thick in consistency.

Whenever body washes are employed to form a foundation tone for pastel, they normally largely disappear as the pastel work is advanced, though there is no set rule about this. Obviously, however, the pastel should predominate in the final effect, though it seldom wholly obliterates the watercolor.

6 / Fixative and Its Uses

While this early experimentation is in progress, you can advantageously familiarize yourself with fixative. This is a colorless liquid which is sprayed upon a completed pastel picture to form a thin, transparent, protective coating to guard the picture from the accidental rubbing or wiping off of the pastel crayon.

We shall speak of kinds of fixative in a moment. As to atomizers, you may use a pressure can containing the fixative, a mouth type blower, or an atomizer with a rubber bulb attachment. The spray can is most convenient, though most expensive. The mouth type, though cheapest, has an annoying habit of clogging. Whichever type you purchase, practice with it for a few minutes until you discover how to produce a fine, uniform mist. Then you should spray a variety of pastel tones experimentally to see how they turn out. Half of a uniformly toned area can be sprayed, for instance, while the other half is shielded from the spray by a sheet of paper; after the fixing, the two halves can be compared. The observing student will thus learn, gradually, in what ways fixative affects the appearance of his work, and also how efficient it is in holding the chalky particles in place.

Fixing the finished picture

Once you have learned to control your spray, you will be ready to fix a finished picture. The customary way is the simplest. Place the picture face up, in a horizontal position, on a table or floor. (Protect the table or floor with newspapers.) Point your atomizer to one side, beyond the picture limit; and as soon as the spray begins, sweep it back and forth across the picture, using a slow, steady motion, always going beyond the picture at both left and right before stopping. Be careful that no heavy drops of the fixative fall onto the painting; to catch any excess drops, an improvised shield of heavy paper can be placed around the opening of the atomizer, or tissue may be held under it. If you do not wish to remove the picture from the easel in order to fix it, a good deposit of spray can be blown directly onto it from a distance sufficient to avoid disturbing the crayon.

Portrait of Peter Freuchen *by Robert Brackman, 16″ x 20″. Private collection. Courtesy, Grand Central Art Galleries, New York. Pastel has always been a favorite medium for the casual portrait which falls somewhere between a drawing and a painting. Note how portions of the face are richly modeled, while other contours are lightly indicated by soft, yet decisive lines. The paper establishes the over-all tonality of the portrait.*

Disadvantages of fixative

Some pastellists object to the use of fixative. They feel that the best treatment for a pastel painting of any importance is to get it under glass or cellophane as soon as possible, without fixing. Their objections, which admittedly have considerable justification, are based on three facts:

1. Fixative, if applied at all generously, dissolves and blends various pigment particles, often changing the color of the pastel work. Light tints in particular may be blended with underlying or adjacent hues in such a way that they are modified in hue considerably. Whites are quite certain to become tinted.

2. Values are also affected, light tones tending to darken.

3. Textures are likewise modified, due largely to the fact that as the fixative dissolves the dry particles of the pastel it unites them, destroying their matte effect.

In short, pastel work, if heavily fixed, sometimes takes on a quite different character from that normally associated with this medium and loses the airy quality which to many is one of its greatest charms.

Advantages of fixative

On the other hand, fixatives are constantly used with great success, and some artists make out a convincing case in their favor. They feel that the loss of this evanescent quality just mentioned is made up, many times, by the development of a more solid feeling of form—an oil painting appearance. To gain such an effect, instead of a single spraying of the fixative on the finished painting, the liquid is applied again and again at intervals as the painting progresses, the pastels being worked in over the fixative, thus creating a heavier layer of color—a so-called *impasto*. This method is generally supposed to have been originated by Degas and used by him in many of his finest pastels.

Another way of applying fixative between stages of painting is to attach an edge of the picture, face down, to a table edge with a piece of Scotch tape, after which the opposite edge can be held by one hand while the fixative is poured over the back of the picture, care being taken to spread it about evenly with a large, flat brush. It will soon soak through the paper to dampen the pastel and fasten it in place. When dry, work can be resumed.

Kinds of fixative

However one applies his fixative, his success will depend to quite an extent on the kind of fixative he uses. There are various kinds on the market, and as a rule any of those especially made for pastel will give satisfaction. Some artists, however—usually the professionals—prefer to mix their own. Fixative, whether commercial or homemade, is manufactured from soft resins (damar, mastic, shellac) and occasionally from Venice turpentine (pitch of larch) or casein. The best fixative is one which both works and evaporates rapidly. A solution of resin with either benzene, ether, or grain alcohol is good. Often ordinary commercial shellac (the "white" has the greatest transparency) is thinned with wood alcohol for a fixative—even the student can make this. It must be remembered that benzene and ether are highly volatile and explosive, and *should never be used near an open flame*.

Mixing your own fixative

If you wish to mix a rapid drying fixative, here are several ways:

1. Dissolve 2% of genuine Venice turpentine (the best is light in color and remains clear in alcohol) in 98% pure alcohol.

2. Thin a 2% solution of white damar with 98% of benzene.

3. Dissolve a 2% pure mastic resin in either alcohol or ether.

For a much slower drying fixative, mix casein with alcohol and water in the following proportions—this recipe is for about one quart: use ½ ounce fresh casein, ¼ teaspoon pure ammonia (not household ammonia), ½ pint of pure grain alcohol, plus water. Soak the casein in 4 or 5 ounces of water for about five hours. Add the ammonia drop by drop, stirring constantly. When the casein has dissolved into a heavy, syrupy mass, add the half pint of grain alcohol and mix well. Add enough water to bring the total to one quart, and filter carefully. If any white substance is found at the bottom after standing, pour the liquid off without disturbing it. If, after testing, the fixative proves too strong in binding the pastel to the surface of the picture, it may be diluted with a small amount of water, though any fixative which is too watery is harmful to pastel.

As a final word, remember that, except for special types of pastel work where fixative becomes, in a sense, a mixing medium, fixatives, whatever their kind, should always be applied carefully and sparingly. Many a good picture has been ruined by their excessive use.

7 / Pictorial Composition

The vital subject of pictorial composition has been treated so adequately by other writers that there seems little point in doing much more here than to direct our readers' attention to its importance.

Definition

Webster defines the word composition as "the art or practice of so combining the parts of a work as to produce a harmonious whole." On the face of it, that sounds very easy. As a matter of fact, some artists seem able to compose almost intuitively. There are others who find that composition is their chief stumbling block.

Unfortunately, composition is a somewhat intangible thing, extremely hard to teach, especially in limited space on the printed page. Composition being an art, rather than a science, there are no definite laws to help; only general principles and practices can be offered.

Elements of a painting

Before discussing a few of these basic principles, let us briefly consider what the elements of a painting—the things that have to be composed—really are. Our first element consists of lines—lines of every kind, shape, tone, and color. Lines scattered at random may be meaningless; the same lines, properly composed, can mean a great deal. Areas of tone are our second element—masses of light and dark of every conceivable form, and ranging in value all the way from the white of the paper to solid black. For our third element, we have innumerable colors of every degree of intensity, and, for our fourth, the textures of the papers and paints. These, then—the lines, tones, colors, and textures —are the elements which must be harmoniously combined if a painting is to be a success.

Your job as an artist is to take these diversified elements and unite them in your painting into a satisfying result.

At the Beach by Burton Silverman, 16″ x 24″. Collection, Dr. & Mrs. Arthur Factor. Courtesy, Kenmore Galleries, Philadelphia. In this richly textured figure study, observe the enormous range of strokes, from the intricate pattern of rounded strokes that define the figure, to the free, almost scribbled strokes of the background which look rather like an abstract painting. The bold strokes of the drapery on the figure's shoulder—which are dashed in and left untouched—are particularly striking.

Unity

As to general principles, a painting must first of all have unity, all parts being so related that they form a complete unit or whole. If a painting gives a homogeneous total effect, it possesses unity, but if it contains disturbing, unrelated qualities or factors, it lacks unity. If an artist is arranging a still life group, for example, and discovers that some object seems entirely out of keeping with the rest, he should omit that object (or modify it in his painting), or his final result will lack unity.

Balance

Our second principle, so closely related to unity that at times the two seem almost inseparable, is called balance. By balance we mean, as the name implies, the equilibrium or restfulness that results from having all the parts of a composition so adjusted that each receives just its correct share of attention. Every part of a picture has a certain attractive force which acts upon the eye and, in proportion to its power to attract, it detracts from every other part. If we find our interest in a painting divided among several parts—if certain lines, tones, or colors seem too insistent—we know that the composition lacks balance. A painting may be "in balance" so far as forms or values are concerned and "out of balance" in color. The opposite is also true.

Balance in a painting is always changing as the artist works. The moment he places a mass on one side of a painting he knows he must counteract it in some other part or parts, not necessarily with an equal mass, but with a mass or masses with like attractive force. In fact, the artist must constantly make such adjustments as he proceeds. When a painting has at last been apparently completed, he must examine it with care to make certain that it is in balance. (If it is reflected in a mirror, faults previously unnoticed will frequently be caught.) If the painting is out of balance, adjustments must be made until every part attracts exactly its proper share of attention in relation to every other part and to the whole.

Emphasis and subordination

This brings us to emphasis and subordination, things which tie right in with balance. Whenever you make a painting, you must consider the relative importance of every part of your subject matter. If one portion seems particularly significant in relation to the rest, this portion should be emphasized. It may be made large in size; contrasting in its light and shade; conspicuous in form, color, or pattern; or perhaps noticeable through its carefully delineated details. The artist must similarly omit or suppress an unimportant part of the subject matter.

Rhythm

Rhythm is another element often sought in composition. By rhythm, we refer to the regular recurrence of similar features—similar trees, hills, or clouds, for instance. Such recurrence is generally pleasing, related forms tending to be more satisfying than unrelated forms. Rhythm is not confined to form; we may have rhythm of value and hue.

Nursing by Harvey Dinnerstein. Courtesy, Kenmore Galleries, Philadelphia. The figures are tenderly painted with light strokes that follow the form with remarkable precision, yet which remain airy and casual. Forms in shadow (like the left arm, the right hand, and the baby's head) are simply patches of halftone.

The Final Touch by Burton Silverman, 32″ x 24″. Collection of the artist. Courtesy, Kenmore Galleries, Philadelphia. A portrait need not be a posed, static subject, but can place the sitter in a realistic setting which tells the viewer about the person's way of life. In this atmospheric study of a woman surrounded by the materials with which she works, the artist has established a mood that tells the viewer far more than would a portrait of the woman alone. Even her gesture is the movement of a person at work in a realistic setting.

The artist as creator

There are many other terms often used in connection with composition—symmetry, repetition, opposition, etc. Whatever the terms used and the principles involved, we can summarize them all by saying that as an artist attempts to produce a work of art he must never forget that he is, in truth, not an imitator but a creator. While nature's subjects will present him with inspiration, they will often consist of a hodgepodge of items, some good in appearance, some bad. Relying on his innate esthetic ability, as tempered by experience, he will exercise his right to select or reject, to rearrange, to substitute, to emphasize or to subordinate, until at last he has translated a bit of the essence of nature into an esthetically satisfying painting.

The beginner will of necessity stick closer to natural appearances. Once he is aware that nature does not concern herself with offering ready made compositions for the artist—that he cannot just set up his easel anywhere and go to work—he will learn to seek some of those agreeable surprises in the form of fine natural pictorial compositions which, with diligence, can usually be discovered.

Geometric composition

There are people who would have the student of nature base his compositions on some geometric plan. And true it is that if we study nature, or paintings by artists of acknowledged standing, we often discover compositions largely utilizing forms which are basically geometric. The triangle, circle, square, and ellipse may all be in evidence. Personally, I feel that for a time, at least, it is best to avoid trying to adopt any definite formulae for composition, and especially any artificial mathematical plan. Instead, you should work simply and directly, following only the dictates of your conscious and subconscious intelligence.

However, I might add that emphasis on certain geometric forms seems to produce definite feelings in the spectator. A picture containing long horizontal lines suggests repose and quiet—as may be seen principally in landscapes—while violently broken lines or color give evidence of unrest and emotional turmoil. Van Gogh, in many of his pictures, affords an excellent illustration of this latter thought. A curving rhythmic line, such as may be seen in numerous Japanese flower and figure prints, produces a feeling of gentle movement. El Greco, through the employment of vertically elongated line and mass, established an aspiring religious motive in his pictures.

Procedure

The student of pastel, anxious to learn to compose, would profit immeasurably by making numerous sketches out of doors, or from the figure or still life, or combinations of these, to clarify his ideas and make himself entirely familiar with his subject. By means of comparative studies he should arrange and rearrange his compositions. At first, these sketches may tend to imitate the subject too closely, or possibly he may prove to be lacking in imagination and inspiration in his attempts to control his efforts; but as he works, he will gradually become aware of his mistakes, and begin to improvise and develop his personal style or vision, which after all is the personality of the artist.

Still Life with Corn Husk *by St. Julian Fishburne. Collection, Mr. & Mrs. Malcolm Stearns, Jr. Courtesy, Davis Galleries, New York. The severe, unbroken shape of the light pot contrasts sharply with the jagged, erratic shapes of the corn husk, which are placed before a darker pot. The dark horizontal line in the foreground, and the bands of light at the top of the picture create an architectural stability in the composition which effectively dramatizes the wild movement of the husk.*

8/Starting With Still Life

At last we are ready to *do* a pastel. We shall start with still life, as this offers the student many advantages. Not only can he find innumerable objects at hand from which to choose suitable subjects, but once he has selected and arranged them, they will stay put, undergoing little or no change in appearance over the period needed to complete his work. In other words, still life offers no distracting movement; animate subjects, on the contrary, are forever moving, and they cannot hold a pose for long. Also, the fact that still life objects are usually represented at approximately their actual size somewhat simplifies the beginner's problems.

The thorough student will want his own collection of still life objects, and will start by gathering those things which appeal to him most—ordinary things, no doubt, like pottery jugs and jars of good proportion and design, and with little or no decoration. Squarish objects, too, such as books, boxes, or baskets, can be employed in composing a still life. He will also find useful a number of pieces of drapery of interesting texture and color, perhaps worn or washed pieces of cloth from old clothing, which, through age and wear, often attain a fine tone. Few new materials have such desirable character.

Selecting and arranging the subject

Do not start with too complicated a subject. Flowers and fruit, unless extremely simple, should perhaps be left until later, though the addition of a bit of colorful fruit or vegetable, plus a leaf or two of interesting shape (keeping all as simple as possible) can vastly improve an otherwise commonplace arrangement. So choose a few simple objects, preferably related by use, shape, or color, so they can be organized into a unified composition.

As the success of your painting will depend to quite an extent on how you arrange your selected objects, give this matter considerable study. Push them about upon your table or other support experimentally, rearranging them, adding or subtracting an item or two, until you have something worthwhile. A viewfinder—merely a card with a small rectangular opening through which you peek, with one eye closed—can be of help, used just as you would the finder on a camera. To repeat, you will soon discover a few well chosen, related objects, tastefully and simply arranged.

Lighting

The direction, strength, and quality of light will help you to determine the ideal arrangement. The light should not, as a rule, come from many sources, as this will

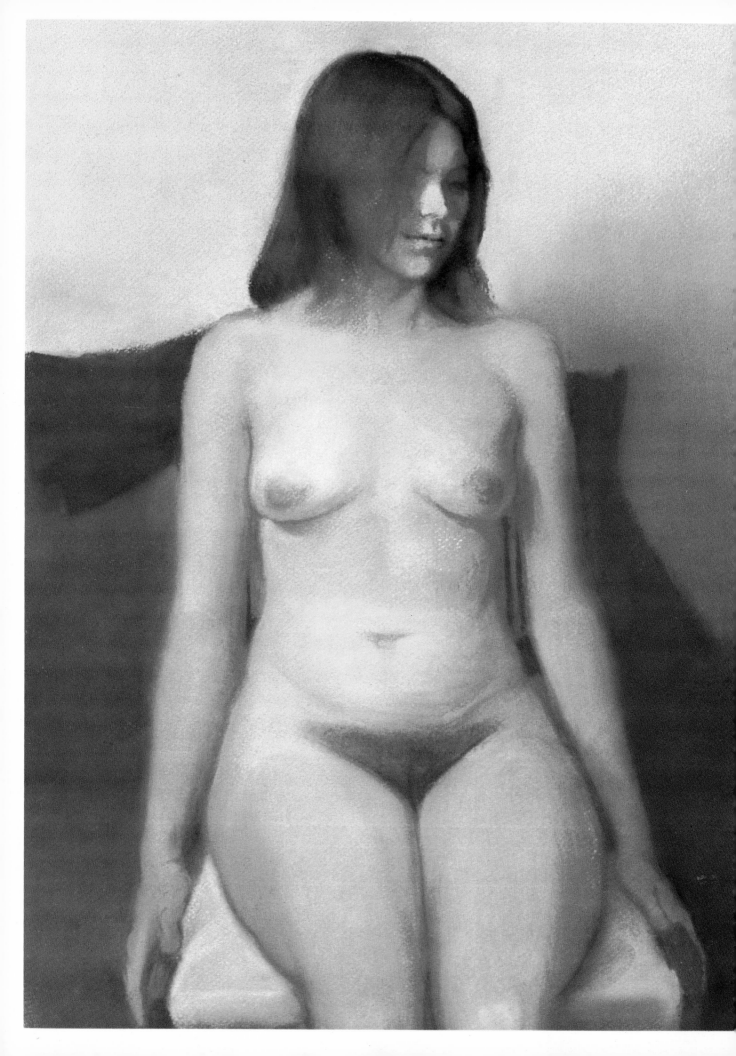

complicate things needlessly. North light is the least changeable of any, and light from a single restricted source—from half a window, or from a somewhat distant window, for instance—is highly desirable.

Thumbnail sketches

At this stage, make a number of small sketches—*thumbnail* sketches is the usual term, as they are but a few inches in size. These should be executed quickly, in pencil, black crayon, charcoal, or pastel, on small pieces of paper. If pastel is selected for the medium, and you prefer to do the work in color, the paper or board for the thumbnails should preferably be the same that you intend to use for the final picture. The sketches will not only help you to arrange your objects advantageously—you must keep asking yourself if your composition is as interesting as it can be—but if you carry them far enough, they will help you to establish, in miniature, the general value and color scheme of your final painting.

Perhaps I should interrupt to point out, rather belatedly, that I am assuming in this entire volume that the reader is interested in what is usually referred to as "realistic" or "naturalistic" representation. Obviously, if his aim is to work along "abstract" or other non-realistic lines, the accompanying suggestions have little value.

Sketching in

With your painting thus planned, you are ready to go to your final paper. The nature of pastel being what it is, do not make the mistake of working in too small a scale. The sketching in can be done with vine charcoal if you wish.

Laying the tone

After sufficient guide lines are established with the vine charcoal, the color tones (lights and darks) are distributed throughout the picture by means of pastels of the correct hue, keeping the whole thing going simultaneously, for if the painter favors one place more than another—that is, works it up in advance of the other sections of the picture—that area may prove to be out of tone (or key) when he comes to finish the remainder. Remember this rule: *keep the whole thing going*.

Shadow interpretation: modeling

The shapes of the shadows, and particularly the edges of shadows as they turn toward the light, should be most carefully observed. The modeling, or the drawing in, of these edges and shapes with the correctly colored pastels, gives the objects their con-

---

Nude *by St. Julian Fishburne, 16" x 12¼". Collection of the artist. Courtesy, Davis Galleries, New York. Painted on buff Ingres paper, this nude was executed in a limited palette of earth colors and blue-grays blended with the fingers and with a stump. Note that the blended areas still retain a subtle texture and are not smoothed out to a uniform, monotonous finish. A single spot of blue to the right of the figure provides a delicate note of contrast to the general warmth of the figure and background.*

struction. There is no smoothing as yet in this second step; the colors are put in as nearly matched in tone to the subject as it is possible to get them by means of pastels selected from the assortment at hand.

Blending

When you have drawn the modeling of the shapes satisfactorily, you are ready to begin blending the tones. The fingers or thumb, tortillons, or stumps—whichever is easiest—are rubbed into the colors, merging them. A remarkable transformation takes place immediately.

The pastels which you have previously applied now attain a beautiful velvety quality; the shapes come together and the painting acquires depth of tone and richness of color.

A pause for analysis: then completion

After you have done this blending, stop working for a short while to contemplate the result. Remove your painting from the easel, slip it into a frame (or a mat cut to fit) and look over its good and bad points before deciding what final work you will do. If by chance you have made the background or the shadows over-dense by too much rubbing, then feathering with the hard sticks of pastel can be brought into play over these passages, breaking up the too flat surface and harmonizing the whole.

Do not, whatever you do, get *too* fussy and finicky over the finish of a pastel painting. When your job is finished it should appear fresh and spontaneous. If certain areas look dull or overworked, do not despair of them; try the feathering process or any other corrective measures that occur to you. You gradually will learn to manipulate your medium so that you can almost invariably rescue even the most hopeless looking results, often in a remarkably short time. No other medium makes possible such amazing changes so speedily. A single touch of bright color, for example, can frequently bring life to a depressingly dull area. A quickly drawn line along a too-much-blended edge can at once restore its definition.

Despite all this, sometimes a result will reach an apparently hopeless state, and you just will not know what to do with it. Often it is best to discard it and start fresh. This is particularly true if you have destroyed the character of your paper. Try the same subject again if you wish—usually it goes much better the second time—or, if your interest has waned, make a new set-up and begin again, remembering, in either case, the adage, "The way to learn to paint is to paint and paint and paint."

Every still life subject will teach you some new lesson—a lesson in form, in tone, in color, in light and shade, or in texture. Therefore, you will want to do many.

It is fun to try different color schemes. In one example, for instance, let the warm colors dominate; in another, the cool. Or one painting can be done in dull, rich, sub-

---

Bouquet of Flowers by Odilon Redon, 31⅝" x 25¼". Courtesy, The Metropolitan Museum of Art, Gift of Mrs. George B. Post. Perhaps the greatest flower painter in pastel was Redon, who carefully contrasted broad, crumbly strokes and textures, with crisp linear accents. As demonstrated here, the whole secret of painting flowers is to think in terms of simple shapes—rather than rendering every petal—and to apply one's strokes directly and decisively to avoid muddy color.

dued colorings, and the next, by way of contrast, in a full gamut of brilliant hues. Study pastel paintings by capable artists; they will suggest color schemes, compositions, technical treatments. By all such means, you will gradually come to a true understanding of your medium.

Flower painting

Flowers are perhaps the favorite still life subject and have exerted a tremendous fascination over the imagination of the artist practically since painting began. Nearly all people love flowers, but the artist, with his keen perception, especially appreciates them. Naturally, no words can give more than a hint of the great variation of impressions which the artist receives from a beautiful arrangement of a bouquet or by seeing flowers in their native surroundings. Their very graceful fragility—their wealth of exciting brilliance—lend a thousand stimulating inspirations to his eye. They challenge the pastellist to do his utmost to capture with his crayons their transient beauty.

However, the beginner, no matter how unbounded his enthusiasm, must exercise some restraint in selecting his first subject for flower painting. For this initial study he should choose a few blossoms of a not too complicated character, such as zinnias, anemones (so aptly called *windflowers*), field daisies, or, perhaps, petunias. He can combine these attractive foliage to make up an admirable subject with which to start.

Flowers often have an amusing, but exasperating, way of teasing an artist. Just when particular pains have been taken to arrange them in their most attractive attitudes—with especial attention to a few important blossoms—and everything seems just right for beginning the work, the pastellist may be quite surprised to observe some of his carefully adjusted flowers slowly turning and twisting themselves out of their original positions and settling down in their own fashion. So, by way of a hint, if the arrangement can be left overnight in the studio before starting to paint, these unruly specimens will have assumed more permanent positions, and this annoyance overcome. Any slight readjustment can then be made before beginning the work.

The best way to paint flowers is to work as quickly as possible on the more important ones, leaving the less perishable materials—drapery, vase, and any secondary accessories—for finishing later. But *do* keep enough color going throughout the whole picture to establish and maintain the general key or tone.

Special crayons for brilliant effects

At this point, a careful selection of the right pastels for flowers is most certainly advised. To the general group, presumably already purchased, there should now be added a number of brilliantly hued crayons, plus a wide selection of greens for rendering the stems, leaves, and any other foliage. These same greens can be utilized later for landscape work. As mentioned before, pastels are manufactured in six tones or more of each color, so, in listing these greens, I shall give the name of the pure color tone only, which in this particular case is Grumbacher's Soft Pastel, Number *D*. There are two tones darker than Number *D*, namely, *A* and *C*; and four tones lighter, *F*, *H*, *K*, and *M*. Of these, *A* represents the darkest and *M* the palest tone. The student may order these, according to his requirements, in half dozen lots of one color, or in single sticks of each color.

Some colors, notably the vermilions and cadmiums, are higher in price than others (the same is true in oil or watercolors), but, by purchasing them in half dozen lots, some saving will be made. I would advise experimenting with a number of pure color pastels at first, and after a trial with these, ordering the lighter or darker hues as needed. As your style develops, certain colors will gradually become your own.

A good list of greens would include: moss green, chrome green (light), chrome green (deep), permanent green, deep green, vert emeraude, olive green.

Add, too, for flower painting, a few half-hard crayons in light yellow and pale tones of green, making it possible to draw the finest lines and so to render the pistils and stamens of any flower whenever these delicate sections are visible.

Accessories

In addition to your pastels and other customary materials, it is well to keep on hand a small number of glass test tubes, plus a roll of narrow transparent cellulose tape. In arranging flowers for a painting, occasionally there will be a fine specimen of bloom with an unfortunately short stem. You will want to use it, but what can you do? Do this: take one of the longer tubes, fill it with water and put the blossom into it; then carefully insert the whole thing into the bouquet just far enough for the surrounding foliage to support it. If this anchorage is not sufficiently secure, take a piece of the tape and hook the tube to a strong stem or sturdy leaf. Also, torn strips of newspaper, inserted at the base of the flowers where they enter the water, make any refractory blooms behave.

If, for additional interest, a piece of drapery is called for in back of your arrangement and you need some support for holding it upright, take two pieces of cardboard about 20″ x 15″, tape the two together in the manner of a book cover, and place one part of this screen in back of the flowers, bringing the other part forward on the side away from the source of light. Hang any desired draperies over this improvised screen. This will simplify the lighting of the flowers, making the shadows deeper, and the whole thing stronger in color values. Such a screen, incidentally, is helpful in many still life arrangements.

Procedure

The procedure in painting flowers is much the same as for still life; the principal exception is that you are now working with perishable subject matter, so the element of time becomes a greater factor. Any preliminary sketches of single flowers, or studies carried out to their fullest detail, will help immeasurably when the time comes for grouping plant material for more ambitious pastels of flowers.

Flower painting obviously need not be confined to interior work; on the contrary, many extremely effective paintings have been made outdoors. In this case it is usually the larger color masses which count, rather than the individual blooms. There is no medium which permits such rapid and effective garden sketches as pastel. Why not try it? Some of the hints in the following chapter may prove of service.

New Paltz in Snow by St. Julian Fishburne. Collection, Mr. & Mrs. William Y. Dear, Jr. Courtesy, Davis Galleries, New York. The feathery softness of pastel is ideal for rendering the atmosphere of this snowy landscape. The distant forms are subtly blended to make them recede, and the clump of trees—crisply drawn with dark lines—steps forward in space with great drama. Although the artist has done a great deal of subtle smudging and blending, the blended areas are enlivened by crisp touches of light and dark.

9 / Landscape

In starting our initial venture into landscape, let me remind the reader that the artist, even if he wished, could not hope to represent truly and completely, with absolute realism, all the brilliant light and color of nature, or all her vastness and intricate detail. Instead, he is at best merely an interpreter, trying to record in a humble way, on the relatively small surface of his paper or canvas, what he feels at the moment to be the most vital attributes of his subject. He omits, he simplifies, he reorganizes, yet always he endeavors to keep the essence of the whole.

One of his main functions is to reduce things in size—an entire mountain, for example, must often be brought down to a few inches in his painting. Obviously this reduction in size calls for a different handling from that normally required indoors, where the subject matter is often represented—this is particularly true of still life—at approximately its actual size.

In view of these new problems, my advice to the beginner is to pick simple subjects at first, and to try to interpret them in simple ways. Even his materials need be but few.

Pastel colors for landscape work

Twenty or so pastels are enough to serve most purposes; here is a suggested selection. Those indicated by number are manufactured by M. Grumbacher.

Vermilion	Bluish-Violet No. 41
Indian Red	Chrome Green No. 62
Yellow Ochre (light)	Deep Green No. 67
Yellow Ochre (deep)	Terre Verte
Red-Gray (Caput Mortuum)	Cobalt Blue
No. 23 (light, medium,	or Permanent Blue
and deep)	Prussian Blue No. 47
Gray-Blue No. 51	Raw Umber

Papers

Colored papers can prove very useful. (If a brown barn is chosen as a subject, for example, a brown sheet of paper will in many instances save time and improve the result.) One should therefore take with him an assortment of papers in medium tones of brown, gray, or green—colors which will naturally lend themselves to an interpretation of stone walls, fences, tree trunks, foliage, and other common outdoor subjects.

Other materials

Here are a number of other items which are necessary for outdoor sketching—plus a few that are optional.

Folding sketching easel and stool
Drawing board, not too large (16″ x 20″ or 20″ x 24″)
Pencils, charcoal, eraser, razor blade, thumbtacks (kept together in a little box)
Small sketchbook
Small cardboard "finder" with opening about 3″ x 2″ for viewing landscapes
Watercolors, gouache, brushes ⎫
Small can for water ⎬ optional

Choosing your subject

With everything in readiness, let us now start together on an imaginary sketching trip. It is a sunny afternoon in late summer. As we walk along, seeking a subject, we realize that the familiar steady gray light of the studio is now replaced by a bewildering scintillation of sunlight playing over all the landscape, and throwing dark pools of shadows under the trees—trees which are alive with shimmering leaves of marvelous greens: olive greens, blackish greens, and hot yellow greens—each tree having its own peculiar structure and character. Great clouds pile up in snowdrifts against the blue of the sky. The hills lie in long, sweeping, rhythmic lines, the grasses under our feet curve and sway in countless patterns, while just beyond the ridge stands a fringe of trees showing the first faint tinge of autumn's red.

You may well stand helplessly asking, "How am I to paint all this? What do I do first? Where do I start?" I have already given you part of an answer in advising you not to attempt too ambitious a subject. Choose something very simple. By "simple" I do not necessarily mean "small," but something not too complex in its form or detail. For your first sketch, you might decide on a single object, or you might like to combine such things as a house, a hill, and a tree, together with sky and foreground. Of considerable help in your selection is the cardboard finder, which is listed among the materials for outdoor work. Held upright, with its opening in either a vertical or a horizontal position, this can be used like the finder of a camera to select either vertical or horizontal compositions.

Do not make your decision as to subject *too* quickly. Walk about a bit. Look in different directions. Pick out the most interesting part of the landscape before you—the part that really appeals to you—and, with one eye closed, look at it through the finder. You will doubtless be most agreeably surprised, as you shift the finder about, to see how subject matter which, without the finder, possibly appeared immense and much too difficult, now is transformed into a picture, or, perhaps, into various individual pictures,

---

The Shepherdess *by Jean François Millet. Courtesy, The Metropolitan Museum of Art, the H. O. Havemeyer Collection. The dominant compositional element here is the cluster of vertical trees, in which the central figure is framed, looming dark against the light sky behind her. This light area is surrounded by the darks of the trees and by the foreground, in which the sheep pick up only a hint of the light that comes from the distant sky.*

at least one of which you will feel confident that you can successfully attempt. As a rule, this subject should not be so near that its smaller details can force themselves upon your attention at the expense of the larger, more important elements.

To most of us, a picturesque old house or a sunlit, weather beaten barn possesses a certain indefinable charm. Such a barn often has, as an added note of interest, an accompanying farmyard life of strutting roosters flashing their vermilion combs, or of horses, cattle, sheep, or other domestic animals. Or there may be inanimate features, such as the mound of a haycock, with its pen holder top, or a majestic silo standing guard over all. An open barn door, with its deep chocolate shadows in the depths, and with wisps of golden hay spilling over the well worn sills, may be enough for one picture—perhaps it will reveal an intriguing farm vehicle half hidden in the gloom.

Such things are perfect subjects for prolonged study, providing a challenge for sound composition and good drawing, and exhibiting not only entrancing hues, but engaging textures to be caught by the pastel crayon. Good, also, are boat houses, fishing shacks, ice houses—in short, almost any man made structures in landscape settings look attractive when recorded on paper with a reasonable amount of sympathy, plus technical skill.

Taking your position

When you have selected your subject and determined the position from which you wish to depict it, you are ready to set up your easel in a comfortable place where the sun does not fall directly on the paper to disturb you. A shade over the eyes or a large hat can prove a big help in protecting the eyes from glare. If it is not possible to arrange the easel so that your paper is out of the direct rays of the sun, then the sun should also be allowed to shine on the pastels in their box, as any great difference in the illumination of the paper and the chalks makes it impossible to judge the colors correctly. In other words, whether you work in a shady or a sunny position, your pastels and paper should be in the same relative light.

Analysis of your subject

You should ask yourself a lot of questions about your subject. What are its leading characteristics? What elements have such appeal that they deserve emphasis? What elements are so distracting or commonplace that they should be omitted or suppressed? What of the colors—do warm or cold colors predominate? Are the colors analogous or contrasting?

Lighting

What is the direction of the light? Does it come from above? From the right? From the left? This direction of light not only determines the shapes of the shadows, but it has a marked effect on their values and color quality. You will notice very quickly, for instance, as you proceed in painting, that, at noontime, when the sun is directly overhead, the shadows are gray and relatively small in size, with clean cut edges, while in late after-

Boris *by Harvey Dinnerstein. Courtesy, Kenmore Galleries, Philadelphia. Dramatically placed against a window, the figure is back lit, with the head silhouetted against the light, and the hand, instrument, and chair delicately defined by an edge of light. The lower part of the figure melts into shadow and is devoid of detail. Only the head is modeled in detail, with careful attention to edges—which are not allowed to become too harsh. The window is thickly painted with rough strokes that allow the darker ground to come through here and there, giving a vibrant effect of light.*

noon the shadows are elongated because of the slanting rays, and are violet hued and softer edged. Early morning shadows are apt to be warmer in color. The shadow forms outdoors, except on dull days, are far more clean cut than indoors, where the light is indirect and therefore diffused.

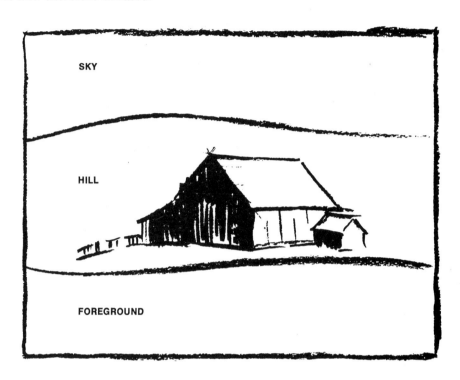

The paper divided into nearly equal parts forms a monotonous design, while an unequal division presents a more interesting arrangement of the component parts.

Composition

When you are ready to draw, some thought should be given to the placement on your paper of your selection of sky, hill, and foreground (or whatever your subject matter may be) in order to make up a pleasing arrangement. That is, you should divide the paper into unequal proportions of sky and hill space, while the addition of a tree or house or possibly a barn would add balance and interest. In order to avoid monotony, none of these objects should be placed directly in the center.

Getting under way

Start your picture exactly as you would a still life, by sketching a few lines in charcoal or pencil to place the subject pleasingly on your paper. Then give a little study to the differences between the colors of the foreground, the hill, the sky, and the object of major interest, whatever this may be. Decide which is the lightest and which is the darkest color in your entire subject. Then proceed to interpret all the various colors, selecting from your box the pastels which come nearest to matching them, and putting a few touches of color in each part of the picture to express nature's color as it appears to you, blending them here and there with the thumb.

It is logical to proceed next with the painting of the sky. Skies are so luminous and scintillating—so flooded with actual light—that even your most painstaking interpretation will be an approximation rather than a true representation. No artist can capture the dazzling brilliancy of outdoor light, but do your best. You will note that sky color, under normal lighting conditions, becomes bluer as it approaches the zenith where the atmosphere is clearest, and paler as it descends toward the horizon. The hill appears darker and bluer in color than the sky; the foreground lighter and warmer.

As we have already hinted, when you come to the painting of the object of leading interest, you must constantly keep in mind not only the intensity of light, but its direction. Also, compare the color of this leading object with that of the rest of the picture, whether lighter or darker, in order to give it its proper place and create a feeling of unity throughout the whole painting. Do not forget that the tone of the paper may approximate parts of the subject. Should this be the case, the paper can often be used to great advantage by leaving these parts free, or almost free, of pastel.

Pausing for analysis

These are only general hints, of course. You will have to let your subject and your mood more or less dictate your procedure. Once you learn that you, the artist, are in a sense a magician, creating on your paper an illusion of those features of the subject which appeal to you, you will have taken a big step in the right direction. To judge your progress in creating this illusion, stand back from your work occasionally—rest your eye by turning to something else for a few minutes—and then, thus rested, examine your work critically. How is it coming along? Does it lack color or tonal contrast? Are some parts too dominant in relation to others? Are your textures too rough or too smooth? Does your painting need to be brought together by working a little of one color into another?

Usually a few minutes of such analysis, now and again, will show you exactly what to do next, and then you will go on to the end, alternating periods of work with periods of analysis. Sometimes your finished attempt may not come up to your expectations and you may feel the challenge to try the same thing over. Good. Go right ahead! Profiting from your recent experience, you are quite likely to proceed far more successfully.

Remember that one of the great virtues of your medium is its adaptability to the quick rendering of the transitory effects of rapidly moving objects—stormy scudding clouds, unusual displays of light and shadow over rolling hills—or of more quiet, low toned evening subjects.

Sketchbook

A pocket size sketchbook should always be kept at hand in which to make thumbnail sketches and written notes concerning the color, light, or other aspects of your subject matter—even the more fleeting and unexpected effects. Later, these notebook impressions can be revisualized in the studio and worked up into pictures.

Some technical pointers

Some pastellists are purists in that they insist on always using pastel by itself, without the addition of any other media. On the other hand, there are those who frequently combine pastel with charcoal, watercolor, or pen and ink. Personally, I can see no objection to any combinations of media, so long as they lend themselves perfectly to the artist's purpose and bring about homogeneous final results. (Obviously, though, in pastel work the pastel medium should predominate.)

Chapter 5 is devoted to various hints on combined media. Just now, I wish to venture a single pointer in this direction—that the landscapist sometimes finds that he can advantageously employ thin washes of opaque color (gouache or pure watercolor) to fill in parts of the picture. When these washes are dry, the pastel can be worked over them to create individual and arresting results.

Do not expect too much

I have already mentioned that you may be disappointed with your first attempts at landscape painting, for it is quite possible that you will expect results which only a more experienced artist could hope to attain. Perhaps even he could not get them! So don't be disheartened if your results look rather amateurish; you will have learned a great deal in producing them. Often one has to practice quite a bit before his results begin to be satisfying.

There is one encouraging aspect! Some of your crudest work, such as the sketchbook notes to which I referred, can often form the basis of satisfactory pastels once you are back in your studio. It is excellent practice to try redrawing some of them in the quiet of your studio while you still hold strong mental impressions of the original subject matter. Your imagination will now have freer reign and you will feel at liberty to recompose your subjects as to proportions and coloring.

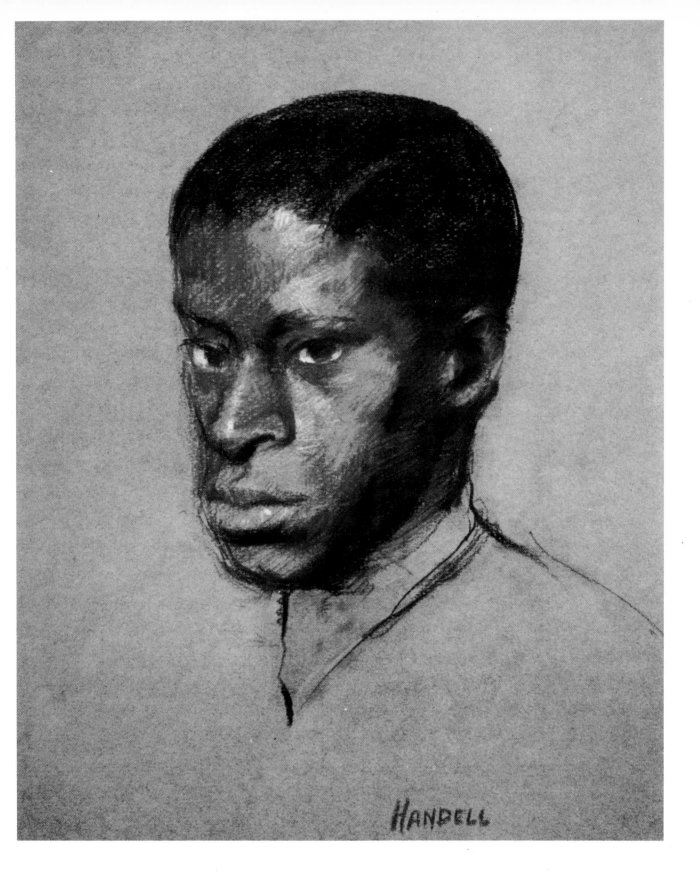

Head of Youth *by Albert Handell. Courtesy, ACA Gallery, New York. This portrait subtly combines broad, painterly strokes with carefully placed linear accents. See how the shadow on the side of the face is first built up in a single broad tone, then overlayed with linear strokes that follow the form. Highlights are judiciously placed and are not overdone.*

79

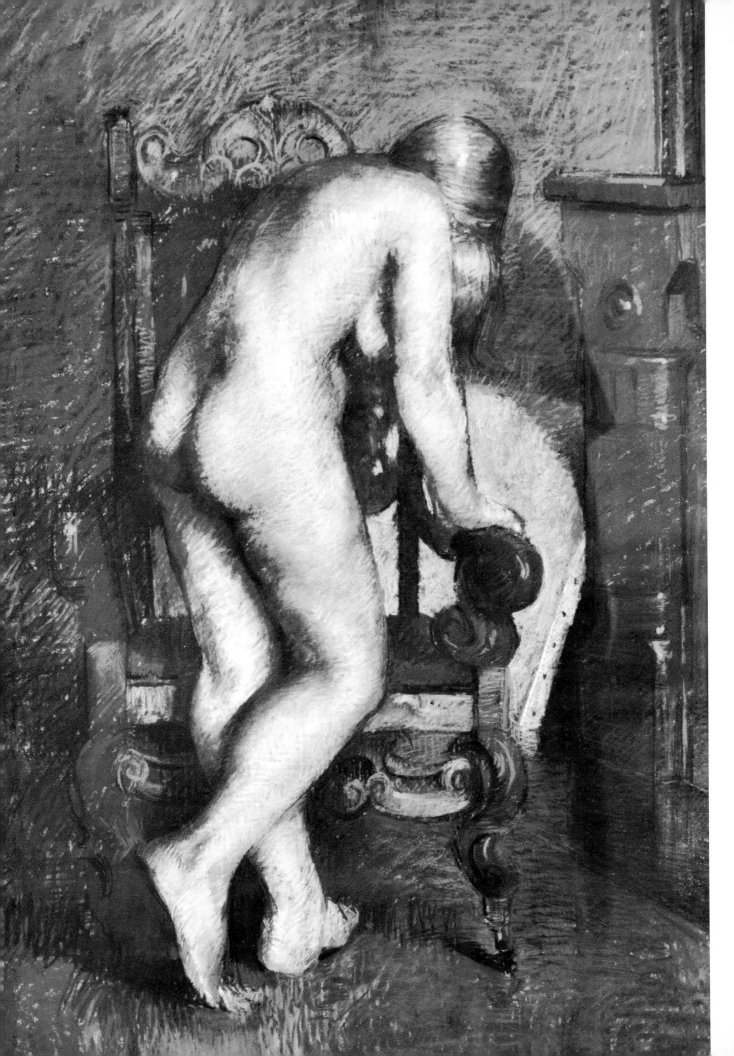

10/Figure Painting and Portraiture

As a preliminary to the treatment of living subjects, we have discussed in previous pages the representation of still life and landscape, as these inanimate things are generally easier to do, and hence seem the natural first choice of the beginner.

This does not mean that the student venturing into the field of pastel cannot turn immediately to animate subjects, such as the human face or figure, if he feels qualified to do so. His main requirement will be a certain surety of drawing without which he cannot hope to interpret with satisfaction the complex proportions of the human body—not to mention its action and other qualities of vitality—or to obtain likenesses of his sitters' faces. Mistakes in drawing which would never be noticed in still life or landscape would be glaring in work from the living model.

Choice of subject

Whether you turn to the living model early or late, you will follow the same basic procedure as was presented in our chapter on still life. First comes the selection of your subject. Usually, whether portraiture or figure work is the intent, your first subjects should be chosen for their marked individuality. Continually be on the watch for types of sitters which so excite you that they make your fingers itch to paint them. For example, for your initial figure study, an old woman would be suitable—one bent with age and with shoulders sloping. Well worn clothes have more character than new, too. For your first portrait study, it would be best to choose a subject with a striking head—perhaps a man whose face possesses strong character lines. An elderly person's face is usually to be preferred (at least for first studies) to that of a younger person, for the youthful roundness and smoothness of facial contour are more difficult to draw, and lack dramatic character.

Posing the subject

With a subject selected, next comes the posing. Here the figure or portrait artist has more freedom, in a sense, than does one working from landscape, for in the open

Standing Nude by Albert Handell. Courtesy, ACA Gallery, New York. The nude has always been a favorite subject of pastellists. The rounded forms of the figure are constructed by a complex series of small, overlapping, interlocking light and dark strokes. Lest the painting should look labored, the background is handled with bigger, freer strokes, and the chair is done in a very sketchy manner.

the subject is usually fixed; one is not privileged to move barns and hills and clouds about until they compose to his liking—at least not in the landscape itself; he may of course do so in his painting—nor can he readily alter the light according to his convenience. Indoors, on the contrary, many elements are more flexible. Not only can he vary the pose until it is just right, but he can control the lighting and arrange backgrounds to suit.

In placing the model indoors, commonplace or stilted poses—people just sitting or standing in stiff or stereotyped positions—should be avoided in favor of more distinctive, though by no means artificial, poses. In portrait work, it is ideal to have your model's head a bit above your own eye level. If you do not own a regular artist's model stand, a packing case large enough to accommodate a comfortable chair will do admirably. If your subject is not a professional model, be sure to pose him so that he is as comfortable as possible; he will then be able to hold his pose for some time without too much effort. Allow enough distance between your easel and the stand (at least five feet) to prevent such distortion of perspective as may occur if you are too close to the sitter.

Lighting

The nature and direction of the light will have much to do with the pose. Take time to adjust the lighting. Usually a simple, one way light is preferred. If the illumination is from two or more directions, the light, shade, and shadow areas may prove extremely confusing in form, value, and hue.

Analysis

With the pose satisfactory, including favorable lighting, do not forget a brief period of analysis; it will pay dividends. Look for the easily recognizable pattern or outline of your subject. No two people are alike, each having his own unique stamp of character, and that character lies in this big pattern.

Try to grasp the most dominant features and then play them up. For example, suppose you have taken for your subject a man well advanced in age. Not only is he stooped and bent, but perhaps his head is thrust forward above a thin neck and his hands lie in his lap, crooked and gnarled. Observe closely how he sits. Note the position of his feet, and how his clothes hang. These are the very signposts showing you his character. So while you are painting him try to express in your work this feeling of age, of frailty. Ignore all the tiny or superficial details until you have caught the big pattern. Then you may add any details that you think necessary.

The Toilette by Edgar Degas. Courtesy, The Metropolitan Museum of Art, bequest of Mrs. H. O. Havemeyer, 1929. The H. O. Havemeyer Collection. This is an extraordinary example of how the direction of strokes can be planned to model form. On the nude figure, the strokes are predominantly vertical and diagonal, in contrast to the broken crosshatching of the drapery on which she sits. The floor is rendered by an open pattern of crosshatched vertical and horizontal strokes. The pattern on the blouse of the servant is particularly worth notice for the way in which the texture of the cloth is rendered.

Detail of La Chanteuse Verte *by Edgar Degas.*

La Chanteuse Verte *by Edgar Degas, 23″ x 18″. Courtesy, The Metropolitan Museum of Art, bequest of Stephen C. Clark, 1960. Degas was fascinated by unorthodox lighting effects. This figure is dramatized by footlights which appear from beneath, and which cast lights and shadows in unexpected places.*

In portraiture, look for the big pattern of the head. Also try to think of the head as a ball. On this ball is a projection—the nose—usually the most prominent projection of the entire head. Naturally, the area above and below the nose will slope backwards, and both sides of the face will round away from this projection.

Getting under way

The artist's analysis is never over. He constantly analyzes both his subject and his painting. From the moment he puts the first strokes on his ground until the work is finished, his subconscious thoughts will run more or less like this: "How thin this old fellow is; his knees almost stick through his trousers. And see how the veins of his hands stand out. I must catch that effect. His hair is very gray and sparse; how can I best show it? And his ears—they look *so* thin and brittle; they are too pink on my painting and too thick. I must improve that." Thus, though the artist concentrates first on the main characteristics of each subject, he must never forget the importance of the contributing detail.

Values and colors: technique

With the proportions of your subject matter right, you are ready to build up the various tones. Look for the darkest shades and the lightest tints, and put them down in the proper hues, in correct relationship one with another. Similarly, apply the intermediate tones.

It is sound technical practice always to keep your pastel strokes running in the natural direction of the contours. This helps you to express the three-dimensional character of your subject, thus obtaining a solid and convincing quality in your work—a quality of relief and projection.

Rest periods

Your model, of course, has to relax now and then, at which times it is best for him to leave the model stand, or at least to change his position for a few minutes. This will give you a chance to rest, too. As a rule, it is advisable for you to refresh your eye by going to the window, or at least by turning away from your work.

Sometimes the artist is glad to take advantage of these rest periods by catching up with the work on certain areas which have fallen behind the rest. As I have repeatedly mentioned, if you can advance all portions of your painting simultaneously, you can judge your work far better than if you complete a part at a time.

Perseverance

It no doubt sounds trite for me to repeat my statement that you can't expect good results without intelligent effort—and plenty of it—but this is true. You must have enthusiasm and the willingness to stay with your work, for drawing and painting from living models are most exacting, and demand untiring application.

You will gradually learn how to get the forms right, the light and shade correct and consistent, your values, colors, and textures convincing, your technique confident yet unobtrusive. You will discover just how to accentuate the essentials (by strong color or value contrasts, by vigorous line work, by detailed handling) and how to suppress or merely indicate the nonessentials. But no one can tell you the proper way to do all this—much depends on how intelligently and persistently you practice.

You can learn much from the illustrations scattered throughout our pages. Original work in galleries and museums also offers a wealth of suggestions.

Memory sketching

Practice making memory sketches. There is no better way to improve your painting. Place the subject—if you have a willing sitter in your family, all the better—at one end of the room and your equipment at the other, facing away from the model. Take plenty of time to study the subject, following the method outlined above; then turn around to your easel and put down all that you can remember from your observation. Now compare your sketch with the sitter. You may be surprised to learn, in your first sketches, how little you really have *seen* of the character of the subject, although you may have been looking at him daily for some years!

Continue to make these practice memory sketches and note your improvement. There is no better training for eliminating fussiness in drawing, a common fault in the work of beginners. By using this method of memory sketching you will learn to grasp quickly the big essentials only, the *pattern*, and avoid what I call inch by inch drawing— a slavish, hesitant copying of your subject set before you. You may of course alternate your work, first drawing from the model directly, and then from memory.

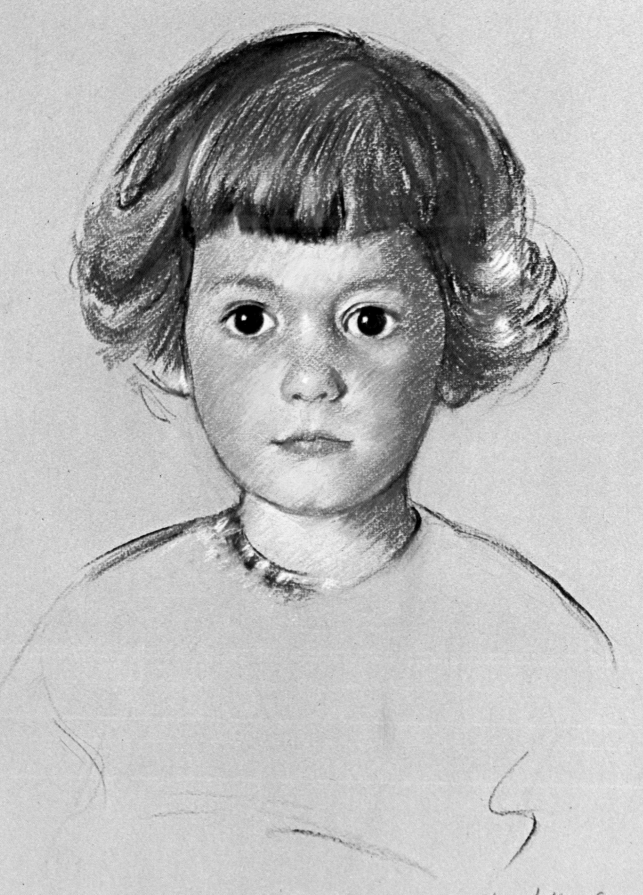

Elinor Lathrop Sears

11 / Children in Portraiture

I write on this topic with particular interest, for the major portion of my lifetime as an artist has been devoted to painting portraits of children. I have done this because I love it, and as a means of earning my livelihood. Fortunate, indeed, is the person who can thus combine his vocation with his avocation. But it is not *all* fun!

The exquisite and all too transient beauty of children can be caught with stunning effect by the pastel. It is the perfect medium to express the appealing sensitivity of a child's face. A child's naturalness of pose, his lack of self-consciousness, his freedom from annoying mannerisms which adult sitters so often display, present a challenge which is hard for the artist to resist. Or it may be the delicate peach bloom complexion, the wistful look, the fleeting, shy smile, or the direct, broad friendly grin of a freckle faced, suntanned youngster that puts one on tip-toe with eagerness to do that child.

But just eagerness for the subject, and a perfect medium of expression, are not enough. One must have enthusiasm, that is true, but an organized approach to child painting is of paramount importance. It is no simple problem to interpret that wonderful evanescent expression of childhood—or, I should say, the countless fluctuating expressions—nor is it easy to portray a body almost constantly in motion, subject to quick fatigue and inattention, on the one hand, and all too ready for active mischief, on the other. Some days the child is at her best, and looks it. Other days the child is not up to par. You, the artist, have to contend with all this and still paint a creditable portrait. Perhaps it will help you if I tell, as fully as one can in print, how *I* do a youngster.

Preliminary preparation

The organized approach that I just mentioned starts in the studio before the child is ever on the scene. If you paint children, you will discover quickly enough that you must await the child, and not expect the child to wait for you! *Patience* is the keystone of such work. I prepare the studio as for an actual sitting—model stand in place, bearing a play table with toys upon it; a folding screen available to put back of the sitter as a support for any needed drapery, or for a pinned up colored paper background; a table nearby on which my pastels are in readiness, along with a sketch pad and small box of watercolors for thumbnail sketches. Last but not least are my easel and the ground of paper or canvas.

Portrait of Kate Rugen *by Elinor Lathrop Sears. Private collection. Pastel has always been a particularly suitable medium for children's portraits because the "bloom" of the medium catches so effectively the peach fuzz quality of children's skin. In this portrait, the ground is cooler than the tones of the head, thereby creating a unifying undertone for the flesh tones and hair.*

Child in Orange Dress by Mary Cassatt. Courtesy, The Metropolitan Museum of Art, Anonymous Gift, 1922. The essence of children's portraiture is softness, but the artist must work with great freedom and decisiveness in order to prevent the softness from becoming cloying. Although the child's face and arms are drawn with gentle, almost indistinct strokes, her clothing and background are rendered with great vigor in large, predominantly diagonal strokes, which give the painting a lively over-all texture.

Detail of Child in Orange Dress *by Mary Cassatt.*

Distribution of light

I give some consideration beforehand to the distribution of the light (which of course varies in both quality and intensity on different days and at different times of day), and keep on hand a number of lengths of black sateen, ready to pin up at the studio window to block out any unwanted light and to strengthen and sharpen the lighting for the little sitter.

Most small children have rather shallow features. The button nose is typical, the bridge of the nose being not fully developed. So a good deal of thought and experimentation should be given to the distribution of light and shade on the subject, forcing the light to key up—to enhance—the beauty and contour of the child's face. Correct lighting gives depth to the eye sockets, strengthens the flatness of a child's face, creates a good strong shadow on the side of the face away from the light for fine modeling of the cheekbones, causes the single brilliant highlight in the eyes for sparkle, brightens the color of the hair, and makes the portrait strong in design and glowing in color.

Too much reflected light results in a weak portrait. Try to avoid double highlight reflections in the eyes (such as two sources of light may create), as these are apt to produce a weak and wandering effect in the eyes. Keep blocking out the light at the window until the subject reveals sharp, strong light and shadow, and a simple highlight in each eye.

Anticipating your mat and frame

Along with the toned papers and canvas, I keep on hand a few picture mats with openings of different size. Some of these mats have oval openings, others rectangular. I study my selected background and the setting through one of these mats, for the opening in the mat is vitally important in helping to place the figure correctly within the allotted area, thus establishing the decorative design of the whole picture.

While on this subject, perhaps I should add that from start to finish I am always thinking, as I work along, of the complete picture—that is, the frame and mat in relation to the portrait. In other words, I do not wait until the portrait is finished before considering its framing. These temporary mats I make of stiff paper or lightweight cardboard, and I suit myself in striping the color bands around the openings to harmonize with the portraits which they are to enclose. Any of the individual color schemes of these temporary cardboard mats can later be duplicated by my framemaker with little trouble; I merely send a sample of the striping.

I also have a rather large assortment of frame mouldings and samples of tinted linens, monkscloth, and pongees. The sample mouldings are numbered for ordering, and my framemaker can easily approximate my fabrics if I show him samples. I am always asking the framemaker for new ideas in mouldings and fabrics which are interesting for portraiture, for I do not like duplications or the use of stereotyped frames if I can avoid them. The really important thing, though, is to have at hand the framing

Danielle *by Burton Silverman. Courtesy, Kenmore Galleries, Philadelphia. In this casual portrait, the artist reveals an important secret about how to keep the surface of a pastel vital and alive. In all the light passages, spaces are left between the strokes to allow underlying darks to break through. Conversely, dark passages are broken by light strokes and hints of underlying light tones.*

materials to mull over, so as to design for each portrait, while it is under way, the most harmonious framing possible. Surely this is logical, for as the mat and frame are to be an important part of the finished work, they should be considered from the very beginning.

Getting acquainted and posing the sitter

With everything in readiness for a prospective sitter whom I am now to meet for the first time, I hang in my mind a large *Do Not* sign to remind me not to pay much attention to the child at this initial contact. I generally keep some little toy in my hand, and casually pass it to the youngster while deliberately avoiding direct attention toward it. Naturally, children are a bit timid with strangers, and a feeling of confidence must be established between artist and child as soon as possible.

As most of the children I paint are under five years of age, they are usually accompanied by parent or nurse, and it is to her that I direct my conversation while the child is left free to roam about, getting acquainted with the studio surroundings. Meanwhile, I am keenly observant of the *first impressions* I am receiving of the youngster, as these impressions are of great importance. I immediately begin to visualize the portrait—how I intend to treat my subject. After a few minutes, the child becomes accustomed to the studio, and it is then quite a simple matter to place her in the chair on the model stand, where, attracted by the play table, she is not aware in the least that she is the center of intense interest and is about to have her portrait painted.

Here I might say that I keep a box of toy junk handy. The youngsters love it. Parts of old flashlights, tea sets, and wind-up toys, most of them well worn by other youngsters. These odds and ends seem to awaken their curiosity and hold their interest more than any new toys could do.

Planning the painting

Taking note of the light again, I select the right background to play up the coloring of the youngster. Perhaps I may suggest a dress of different color, or a change in the collar design. On the other hand, it is sometimes surprising to find how much sentiment is attached to a special garment which the parent likes on the child. Naturally, I try to accommodate the parent in this respect, providing that the dress is paintable and attractive. For, after all, it is to be the parents' portrait to live with and enjoy. But I try never to make the clothes too obvious. It is the child's head that the spectator should see when he views the portrait, and too fussy and elaborate clothes will detract rather than add.

Young Woman with Muff *by Auguste Renoir, 20¾″ x 14¼″. Courtesy, The Metropolitan Museum of Art, bequest of Mrs. H. O. Havemeyer, 1929. The H. O. Havemeyer Collection. In this very delicate pastel, the great French artist uses the chalk primarily as a linear drawing medium, rendering the face and clothing with crisp, light strokes, much as he would draw with charcoal. On the jacket, the color is applied broadly, then overlayed with light and dark strokes that follow the rounded form. In the background, he has freely scumbled a light chalk over the toned paper, which is allowed to show through to produce a lively effect.*

Also at this first sitting I discuss with the parent the number of sittings required, which will depend a good deal on the age and tractability of the child. Unless I have previously done so, I likewise make the business arrangements connected with the commission price of the portrait, settling on how much is to be paid, when it is to be paid, etc. There should be nothing vague about this, to cause later misunderstanding.

Not until then do I make my usual quick thumbnail sketch or two, putting in the color notes with watercolor or pastel. This generally terminates the first sitting. I also explain that, for future sittings, I prefer to work with the child alone.

Working alone with the child

My primary reason for working alone with the child, whenever possible, is that most adults, although well meaning, are apt to be distracting influences unless they are accustomed to portraiture procedure. In the case of an adult's first studio experience—remember it is usually the mother or the nurse who comes—she is very likely, just as I am ready to put down an important observation, to distract the child's attention by insisting that the child look at me. Consequently, at that crucial moment, the child looks at the speaker and not at me. And that ubiquitous comb! A comb always seems to pop out of nurse's pocket to smooth her charge's hair at exactly the time when an interruption is least desired. That vibrant and interesting moment is lost!

So, by diplomatic means and otherwise, I try to dismiss these well intentioned guardians from my studio room, turning them either into the garden outside or into the anteroom, so I can have the child to myself.

After the first sitting and a few minutes' rest, the child is keen to return and play at the toy table, and she will generally settle down very readily and forget about the nurse or parent. During the actual sittings, I let the youngster play at the table as she wishes, and attract her attention by talking to her or by making my singing bird perform—an absolutely dependable attention getter. Perhaps I clown for her, and put a daub of colored chalk on my nose. My toy telephone (a piece of string with a metal disk at each end) is another source of great amusement. I keep one end hanging on the back of the easel and talk over it to my little model. The surprised and delightedly animated expression when she hears my voice through the disk, which she holds to her ear in imitation of me, is just what I want to record.

Fatigue is a thing to guard against. A young child tires quickly, and so, at the first sign of restlessness, the sitting is over. Down she comes off the model stand and out into the garden for a rest, until she sits again. She is generally very willing to return to the play table after a few minutes' relaxation. The number of sittings required before a portrait is completed varies with the temperament and the age of the sitter, and the way in which the painting develops. I normally count on five sessions in all, each totalling an hour or an hour and a half. That is a fair average.

After the Bath by Robert Philipp. Collection of the artist. Courtesy, Grand Central Art Galleries, New York. In pastel painting, the surface of the paper, board, or canvas plays an especially vital role. The loosely applied tones of this figure allow the warm hue of the ground to come through. The background is left untouched, the color of the support being sufficient. It is worth noting that the shadows on the flesh are frequently cool, rather than warm, and that the artist has developed a subtle interplay of cool and warm tones in the shadow areas of the figure.

Details of portraiture

Now, at last, we are ready for the details of making a portrait. I have posed my young model and am satisfied with the lighting. I have made a number of thumbnail sketches and have selected the one which I believe to be the most expressive of the child's character. I begin the actual portrait by sketching the proportions lightly with charcoal, commencing at the top of the head. (I like to work life size in portraiture of children, and most of my portraits are of this size.) Then, working downward, I suggest the tones of the hair—the darks and lights in the right places—and leave the finishing of the hair until later. I try to sketch the eyes as soon as possible at this sitting, and indicate lightly the position of the nose and mouth.

Eyes

The old saying that the eyes are the windows of the soul seems never more true than when you look into the face of a child. The expression which lies in the eyes makes up half of the portrait, and the closest possible attention must be paid to them in order to portray them as expressively as possible.

While I am engaged in placing the eyes correctly, I sketch in the bone shadow of the nose between the eyes so as to give a feeling of depth. Otherwise a misleading flatness may occur in this region to throw me off. Then I go directly to painting the eyes. In the simplified lighting which I have arranged, there is plenty of color in the iris, whether the eye be dark or light. I attract the child's attention, and observe carefully the exact position of the pupil of the eye. Often the two pupils are not on the same level. I strike these in with black pastel. (Be sure you have a fine jet black for the pupil. Some blacks on the market are of a dull grayish tone, entirely unsuited to this purpose. A good black is rather hard to find. Grumbacher has one that is satisfactory.) I then place the exact position of the single highlight in each eye, putting it in with a stick of white pastel, the half-hard type preferred. These highlights should be crisp, direct, and sure.

I take plenty of time for these two observations, bearing in mind that this is where so much of the child's sparkle and animation lie. I add a touch of Prussian blue over the black pupil to give it greater depth, and I use vine charcoal and a bit of pastel black to draw in the rim of the iris if it has a very definite rim. I finally blend the color of the iris, in case it needs darkening, with the charcoal, stroking the soft charcoal gently over the pastel. (Most blue eyes, however clear and pure their color may appear, show a slight tone of gray-green, so do not paint your eyes as blue as delftware. If you do, they will only jump from the picture and appear out of key with the rest of the head.)

The Brothers *by Burton Silverman. Courtesy, Kenmore Galleries, Philadelphia. One of the unique qualities of pastel is that it bridges the gap between drawing and painting; it can be used as a drawing medium, a painting medium, or something in between. This sensitive study of two boys comes closer to our definition of drawing, rather than painting, because of the emphasis on line and because the pastel is used very lightly as patches of tone interspersed with linear definitions. Aside from the shadow beneath the figures, the background is untouched.*

Eyelashes

Eyelashes come in for special attention. Seldom do children have lashes dark or heavy enough to be rendered in pitch black. The light skips over the eyelashes and tends to give even the darkest of them a deep reddish-violet color. I use a Caput Mortuum, deep (Grumbacher) here, and a touch of vine charcoal, and strengthen the line. The deepest black should be in the *pupil* of the eye and not in the eyelashes. *Never* paint eyelashes one by one, movie actress fashion. This cheapens any pastel portrait and proves the artist to be incompetent in drawing the eye properly in its surrounding socket. You will notice that where the eyelash goes over the iris and pupil, it appears darker; so strengthen this line carefully with a bit of charcoal or Prussian blue, or, if you must, with black pastel.

Keeping the whole portrait going

To bring the painting to life as soon as possible, and to keep the whole thing going, I like to strike in the color note of the dress, a bit of carnation in the cheeks, the highlight on the nose, or suggest a little color in the lips. It's surprising what just these stenographic notes of color will do to help one get the feeling of the whole portrait.

I work in the cheekbone structure next, on the side away from the light. Then I place the ears, and snap in the darkest shadows in the nose with gray-green and, in the deepest part, with the reddish-violet already mentioned. This projects the nose structure, and the roundness of the face begins to take form.

Nose

The button nose of a child is full of color. Delicate shell pinks and yellow ochre make up a good deal of the color in the lighter parts. I model the nose rather fully because of the shallowness of the undeveloped bridge. Then when the lighter parts and the shadow side are complete, I soft pedal the bridge shadow by whisking my thumb across it, lightening and blending this small area. A too pronounced shadow here at the bridge is likely to age the child's expression, so I do not overdo it. The shadows at the button end can be left full strength for structure, but should be checked with the shadow of the cheekbone for correct value of tone. The deepest shadow on the nose will approximate the darkest shadow of the cheekbone.

Rest period

At about this point, it is usually best to take time out, for I have been working at top speed, and a general checkup of the portrait is advisable. Perhaps the child is through sitting for the day, and that will give me time to look the portrait over thoroughly before her return. I rarely work without the sitter for the important features, but a bit of memory painting can be done when she is absent, especially in toning down any over modeled sections. A soft whisk of the thumb will often bring too pronounced modeling into a perfect blending of contour. But I use this blending with discretion, so as not to weaken the modeling by over blending; I wish to keep the pastel crisp.

Sleeping Youth *by Albert Handell. Courtesy, ACA Gallery, New York. Much of the charm of pastel is its ability to suggest more detail than is actually there. Most of this figure consists simply of flat, dark tones; the form emerges with the addition of a few crisp light and dark strokes to indicate folds and to model the form very casually. The face and hands are handled with a minimum of detail, and almost without crisply defined edges. The background is literally an abstract pattern of strokes.*

The big shadow of flesh and bone on the dark side of the head comes next, and I work this along with the color tones of the lighter side. The exquisite color in the edge of the cheekbone shadows, as they turn into the light, must be noted, and I compare the flesh tone of the face with the neck, which usually lacks the rosy color of the face but has a fine warm creamy color distinction, and a good deal of olive green in the shadows.

On the light side of the face and forehead I carefully model the flesh tones, and note the brilliant shell-like color of the ear. The lobe is generally lighter and brighter in key than the cheek, which turns back toward it.

Mouth and chin

I have already indicated the position of the mouth, and perhaps have put in a few touches of color. Now I am ready to give it my entire attention for, next to the eyes, the mouth is the feature most indicative of the child's character.

Here the keenest observation is brought to the test, for out of all the different expressions of the mouth I now have to decide which is the one that is most typical of the child. It may be the gentle shy smile of a little girl, or the bubbling over grin of a boy, but that fleeting expression must be caught accurately and quickly. The upper lip will be cooler in color and darker than the lower lip, and if the mouth is closed, the center line between the lips will be richer and darker than all the other parts. I look for the little quirks in the corners of the mouth, and the pattern of shadow that surrounds the bulge of the lips on the side away from the light. There is a lot of cool gray-green in the shadows around the mouth, and a bit of light violet pastel is used on the side toward the light to round the lower cheek and chin down under.

The shadow on the neck should be strong in value to support the head (project it), and a little reflected light is generally seen on the jawbone above this big neck shadow. This gives roundness to the cheek, and I draw this in with a half-hard pastel.

When the head is about this far along, I recheck the values throughout and blend any parts that are too jumpy in value. I next give attention to finishing the hair.

Hair

During all the time that I have been working on the other parts of the portrait, I have kept on the watch for the moment when the child's hair would appear at its best. Hair is as individual as handwriting. Its springiness and direction of growth, its texture, and its color are the essentials to look for. I wait for the day when the child's hair is just "wonderful" and then I go to work posthaste to strike it in as quickly as I can.

Not all children are blessed with lovely hair, but you can make any hair interesting in pattern and texture. Boys are a problem particularly—their ears *will* stick out unpleasantly if they have too short a haircut. And, by way of a hint or two, when you start a portrait, try to persuade the parent *not* to cut the child's hair until you are through.

Pregnant Woman *by Burton Silverman. Courtesy, Kenmore Galleries, Philadelphia. Despite the gentle nature of the subject, this study of a pregnant girl is painted with almost ferocious vigor. Big, ragged strokes of color race across the paper; the strokes create patches of color and model the form only in selected areas like the head and hands. Strangely enough, the ragged finish enhances the tender mood of the subject.*

Nothing can be more disconcerting than to see a freshly shorn head to paint, in place of the one you have already sketched in. The other hint is to keep the parent from slicking the child's hair down. It will only give a set, unnatural look to the portrait. I like to paint youngsters' hair just as it is when they come into the studio after a little run in the wind, which has given a sort of breezy lift to it.

So when the time comes to do the hair, I put in all the darks and lights and plenty of color, too, for hair has lots of color. Afterwards I thumb-whisk the pastel together rather solidly to give it a fine sheen and texture.

For general use in painting dark hair, the following pastel list is useful: Prussian blue, olive green, reddish-violet and reddish-brown for the darks; cadmium orange, yellow ochre, light blue, and violet for the intermediate tones and lighter sections. In blond types of hair, there are violet, blue and gray-green in the shadows, while light greens, lemon yellow, pale cadmiums, and light flesh pink make up the color and highlights.

Clothes and accessories

When it comes to the question of clothes and accessories, the artist must remember that while they must not be too obvious, just as much thought should be given to their design and color in the painting as has been given to the head. Clothes can add immeasurably to the decorative feeling of the picture, and a certain delightful pictorialness in children can be brought out by the right choice of costume.

When a tiny ash blond child, dressed in a blue-green poke bonnet and a slender fitted coat, is brought to the studio, I can see her painted only in that hat and coat. And I emphasize her Frenchiness and femininity by posing her against a background of pale salmon pink to bring out her exquisite fragile coloring and tiny waist. Or perhaps it may be a boy, who could have stepped out of the eighteenth century, in a frilled collar and pink linen suit. When these "picture" children appear, I give my imagination full play in painting them. On the other hand, the rough and tumble boys in pullover jerseys, and the little girls in pinafores, plaids, and pigtails come in for their full share of my interest. It's fun and exciting to paint all of them.

Summing up

It is hard to say just what makes a good portrait. Certainly a satisfactory likeness is the first requirement, but just a likeness does not make a fine portrait. Beyond his technical skill, the artist, if he is to paint a portrait which is convincing and alive, must have a sympathetic understanding of his subject and an acute psychological insight into the character of his sitter.

There is often a marked difference in the way in which the artist and the parent perceive the same child—the child has one appearance to the parent and quite a dis-

The Actress by Aaron Shikler. Courtesy, Davis Galleries, New York. In this delicate portrait of a child, the artist contrasts closely knit strokes that build up the form of the child's head and arms, rough strokes that build up the impasto of the bed behind her, and wispy strokes for her gown. This is a particularly good example of pastel's special ability to capture intricate light effects.

similar one to the artist. An adjustment can (and must) be made to the satisfaction of both. I paint a child on the premise that the parents have selected me because they like my way of doing children. Otherwise they would have gone to someone else. It has been my experience that parents are only too willing to get the artist's viewpoint of the child, for that was what originally attracted these parents to the artist.

But I do realize that this may be their initial experience in the field of portrait painting—quite likely it is—so, at the first sitting, I explain how I intend to paint their youngster. After that, I do not expose the portrait until it is well enough along in likeness for them to understand it. If a portrait is shown too early, the unfinished technicalities and blank portions tend to confuse them. If, after viewing the portrait, a parent suggests some changes, I talk over the suggested changes with both parents, if possible, and perhaps compromise on certain points.

You must not expect that all your portraits will go along smoothly. There will be many discouraging moments, and you will wonder why you ever chose to be a painter of children. But if you will remember that your painting eye has its good days as well as bad, the same as your young sitters do, and if you stick to your job, you will ultimately acquire success and you will have immense satisfaction in making pastels of children— one of the most difficult but most fascinating types of subject matter in the world of painting.

Portrait of the Artist *by Robert Philipp. Courtesy, Grand Central Art Galleries, New York. Surprisingly, this lively self portrait was painted on corrugated cardboard. The strong vertical texture of the board enlivens the entire painting. Except for the face, which is painted with small, but free strokes, the painting is executed with casual, scribbled strokes, which are lightly blended, but never allowed to disappear altogether.*

108

12 / Matting, Framing, and Hanging

Whenever a pastel painting is completed, the question at once arises as to how to safeguard it from damage. Surely it cannot be left lying around unprotected, or it will soon be ruined either through accidental rubbing or by acquiring a coat of dust.

Fixing, storing, mounting

In Chapter 6, I discussed at some length the use of fixatives, pointing out that unless they are employed as an aid to the technical development of a picture they should preferably be used sparingly, if at all, inasmuch as any fixative, no matter how clear and pure, will alter to at least a slight degree the appearance of a pastel painting. (The common fixatives used for charcoal are perhaps the worst offenders, often having a noticeable effect on the colors.)

Whether a completed painting is fixed or not, if it is not to be framed at once it should be laid away in safety. It may be placed face upward in a portfolio (the latter laid horizontally), with a protective sheet of cellophane, clear plastic, or wax paper covering it, and kept until wanted. Any number of pastels may be piled in this way without danger, providing they are carefully handled.

Some artists mount their pastels after they are made. The method used is much like that employed for mounting blank pastel paper, though extra precautions must be taken to protect the face of the painting.

Pastels need not be mounted before framing unless one wishes, although it is quite a common practice to do so. Artists often rely on professional picture framers for such work; not all framers, however, are qualified to relieve the artist of this particular detail.

Mats

As to mats, many materials are suitable, ranging all the way from plain cream or white pasteboard to fabrics of numerous types. There are elaborate French or Empire mats, decorated with fine lines of colored ink and bands of gold passe-partout tape. These are ideal for pastel portrait work which demands a surrounding tone to tie in with the portrait scheme. The framer makes them to order from the artist's designs.

Nude *by Albert Handell. Courtesy, ACA Gallery, New York. This solidly painted figure and geometric background are composed of a network of boldly crisscrossed strokes which create a lively, integrated surface throughout the composition. Observe how the strokes on the hair and torso follow the form around, while the vertical strokes on the floor paradoxically contrast with the horizontal plane, yet make it lie flat.*

Of the fabrics used for mat making, pongee, rayon, coarse or fine linen, and silk in neutral or delicate tints form a group to excite the eye of the pastellist—they offer variety in both texture and color. For a strong picture, neutral monkscloth, combined with a narrow insert or fillet of white or colored pasteboard, makes a bold and unusual mat. As mentioned before, I plan my mat and painting at one and the same time, so the two (when completed) form a unified whole.

Framing methods

There are three basic methods of framing a finished pastel. In the first, a deep sunk or *box* mat is fitted to a wooden frame to keep the picture well away from the glass. In the second, no mat is used, but four narrow strips of wood are glued to the inside of the wooden frame between the glass and the picture, to prevent the picture from coming into contact with the glass. In the third—which is a good method for the temporary exhibition of pastels—passe-partout tape is employed.

Passe-partouting

In passe-partout work, the picture, with or without a mat, is gently laid face down against a piece of glass of its exact size. A cardboard backing, also of the same dimensions, is next laid against the back of the pastel. Then, using the greatest care to prevent any slipping, the framer moistens and applies previously cut strips of passe-partout tape around the edges of this "sandwich," leaving the tape to show on the face of the glass for about $\frac{1}{2}''$ all around, to form a uniform margin, and wrapping the tape carefully around to the back. This method seals all the edges together, keeping out the dust. In a completed passe-partout, no movement should be possible. Special hangers are available for this type of mount—these should be used as directed by the manufacturer.

Returning to the matter of wooden frames, simple mouldings of wood, waxed or finished in metal or gold leaf, perhaps with a small amount of decorative carving, are an excellent choice for pastels. If one is doing the backing of the frame in the studio, having the finished frame on hand, it is a good idea to give the mounted pastel painting a light sharp tap on one edge (just before framing) in order to dislodge any loose particles of pastel which might otherwise eventually fall off between mount and glass.

Framing directions

Here are some definite framing directions. First, the glass (which should be picture frame glass, not window glass) goes into the frame; be certain that the glass is spotless. Insert the mat next to the glass, fastening it to the inside of the frame with a few brads to keep it secure. Cut several small strips of gummed paper tape or linen library tape—never masking tape or Scotch tape, which stain permanently. Then take the mounted pastel (or unmounted, as the case may be), and fasten it to the back of the mat across the top only, with the aid of the tape, allowing the bottom to ride free in the frame. This prevents any buckling such as the pastel might otherwise be subject to, in case of dampness. The water soluble glue on the tape allows the removal of the pastel quickly if a change of frame is wanted.

With the pastel in its final position, place a piece of thymolized paper (Chapter 13), cut to glass size, over the back of the pastel, and insert a heavy cardboard backing or a three ply wooden back board. (Such plywood, incidentally, should be free from knots and blemishes.) If cardboard backing is used, it is fastened in place with small brads, but plywood is cut to full frame size and screwed into position for, naturally, hammering should be avoided so far as possible. If a blanket is laid on the work table, and the framing process is carried on over this, shock will be reduced to a minimum.

Paper strips about two inches wide may now be glued over the brads and the back of the frame moulding on all four sides to keep out dust and dirt. It is not necessary to cover the entire back with paper except for appearances' sake; there is even some doubt of the advisability of doing this because of the possibility of attracting dampness.

Esthetic considerations

Turning from the practical to the esthetic, the first principle in choosing a good frame is suggested by the question, "Is it suitable?" By *suitable*, we mean harmonious in size, tone, color, and texture, so that perfect unity will be created between the picture and the frame.

Obviously, the frame should not attract too much attention to itself—it is really a sort of transitional member between the picture and the wall, serving to emphasize the former and to set it off slightly from the latter. If the picture exhibits a bold type of subject matter, a blatant technical treatment, or a strongly contrasting color scheme, it may call for a correspondingly heavier frame than would be selected for an unobtrusive picture. In other words, one should avoid bold or conspicuous frames for fragile, refined treatments, or unemphatic subject matter, and vice versa.

Plain frames are *always* safe if they are of appropriate color and texture—they will never detract from the subject matter.

Hanging pastels

As to hanging, there is little that we can offer beyond recommending careful adherence to the rules of good taste.

One important thing is to make certain of proper lighting. Inadequate light, or light from the wrong direction, causing strong reflections on the glass, can throw even the best of paintings into eclipse.

Another point is to see that the picture is hung against a suitable background—one which is not so full of riotous color or design that the picture has to fight for supremacy. Similarly, competing paintings should never be hung adjacently.

As to color, if some of the colors of the painting can be repeated, possibly in a softer key, in other parts of the room—perhaps the walls, rugs, draperies, or upholstery fabrics —that will tend to make the picture seem part of the entire decorative scheme. Every effort should be made to make the painting belong.

As we shall see in the next chapter, pastel paintings, like paintings in other media, are subject to diseases, mainly due to dampness. It is a wise precaution, therefore, to hang pastels on inside walls, or on those which are *known* to be dry.

13/Preservation of Pastels

When pastels are carelessly hung on damp walls, or stored in humid, badly ventilated places, they become subject to mildew—in fact these conditions are ideal for the development of this damaging fungus. This is because paper is hygroscopic, that is, tending to absorb and retain moisture. Therefore, wherever such conditions exist, all pastels should be inspected frequently for such growths. Mildew may be recognized readily by the fluffy gray spores (mycelium) lying like small islands of dust on the surface of the pigment or on the paper itself.

Treatment for mildew

When a pastel is found damaged by mildew, the painting should be removed from the danger area, and, if already framed, the back should be opened and the picture taken out for the following treatment. Place the picture on a flat surface. Pick off the fluffy growth with a soft camel's hair brush which has previously been dipped in pure grain alcohol. (Care should be taken that the spores are not scattered about to cause further damage.) If the mildew is deep seated, a delicate scraping with an edge of a razor blade may be necessary. Touch infected spots lightly again with the brush and alcohol; this will sterilize them. They can then be concealed easily by touching them up with pastel to harmonize with the surrounding areas. Reframe the pastel painting, placing a sheet of thymolized paper in back of it before the back boarding is sealed in place.

Thymolized paper

Thymolized paper is prepared by soaking white blotting paper in an alcohol solution of thymol crystals. These may be purchased at a drugstore, and should be of 10% strength. The solution should be freshly made before treatment is begun, and the alcohol should be allowed to evaporate from the paper before use. A stronger solution can be made by melting the crystals into the blotting paper, or into a pile of papers, by pressing with a hot iron.

Figure in Blue *by Aaron Shikler. Courtesy, Davis Galleries, New York. In this vertical composition, the artist concentrates his darks in the lower half, and his lights in the upper half, placing the figure where the dark and light halves of the picture meet. Note how the light side of the figure is placed against a dark background, and the dark side of the figure against a light background. The strokes of the light background are free, almost random, in contrast to the more intricate handling of the figure.*

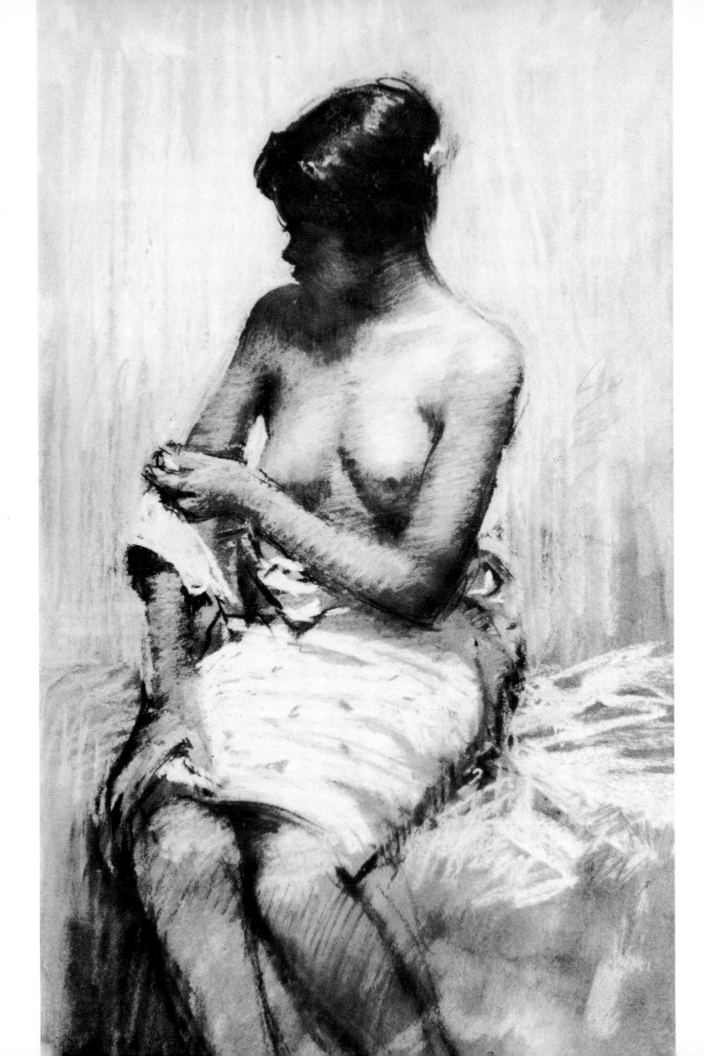

These treated papers can be interleaved occasionally into a portfolio of unframed pastels to prevent the development of mildew. Thymol vapor cannot remove mildew once it has formed; it acts as a preventative only. No permanent immunity can be expected from sterilization by it, so freshly prepared papers must replace the old ones every few months.

Ultramarine disease and treatment

Under certain unfavorable atmospheric conditions, the valuable pastel color known as ultramarine is gradually injured by acid vapor, or bleached by weak acids. This is true of both the genuine lapis lazuli and the artificial product (generally used today) made by heating clay with various compounds. (Pure artificial ultramarine pigment is in itself nonpoisonous and permanent; but we are concerned only with its preservation in pastel form, where it is one of our most beautiful and useful colors.)

Ultramarine has a tendency to hygroscopic action, doubtless because of its heavy clay base, and frequently a whitish film will develop over its surface in a pastel painting —the so-called *ultramarine disease*. The affected picture should be removed to a drier atmosphere and treated the same as for mildew. If it is absolutely necessary to rehang it in its former location, which is suspected of being damp, pieces of cork should be fixed at all four corners of the back so that the picture hangs away from the wall, allowing free ventilation around it. Even with this precaution, frequent inspection is necessary to check any possibility of further disease.

Preservation of unframed pastels

Unframed pastels can be stored on horizontal, rack-like shelves, which allow proper ventilation, whether the paintings are in portfolios or resting on heavy cardboards. Each pastel should have its own protective cover of cellophane, clear plastic, or wax paper. Small mesh bags containing thymol crystals can be hung at intervals, or laid on the corners of the shelves, close to the pictures. If portfolios are used, they should be propped open occasionally to allow air to circulate through them, and the pictures should be inspected for possible mildew.

It cannot be too strongly emphasized that dampness and its attendant ills are the greatest causes of destruction to pastels.

Woman Dressing *by Burton Silverman. Courtesy, Kenmore Galleries, Philadelphia. Much of the charm of pastel lies in the artist's ability to decide when to stop. The greatest pastels often leave many portions of the painting unfinished. In this intimate study of a girl, only the torso is carried anywhere near to completion; from the waist down, the figure is barely drawn, and merely accented with light and dark touches to suggest light and shade. Note how the face and shoulder blend into shadow, with the chin completely undefined.*

14/Painting Portraits As a Profession

Many people with aspirations along art lines have asked me at one time or another what I think of portrait painting as a profession. It seems logical to anticipate that this query will arise among my present readers. Hence, I will try to answer it. Briefly, I can only point to the obvious fact that if I did not think highly of portrait painting, I would not have gone on with it for all these years.

About compensation

Some even question me bluntly as to how much remuneration the artist can hope to expect from painting portraits. Who can say? Much depends on the skill of the individual artist, on his opportunities for exhibiting his portraits to the public, and on the response of the public to his work. If the reaction is favorable, many people will ultimately want their portraits painted. So, if an artist is good—good enough, at least, to do acceptable work—he can certainly earn a satisfactory living in normal years and have a fine time doing it.

I realize that different people have quite divergent ideas as to what constitutes a "satisfactory" living. Surely no one could earn more than a decidedly modest income by sketching "likenesses" for five or ten dollars each (unless he did them by the hundred), and no buyer could expect much for such a sum—not real portraits! But there are numerous people who, in normal times, would gladly pay for capable portraiture anywhere from one or two hundred dollars (to mention a bottom price), to as many thousand, depending on the skill and reputation of the artist. If the painter's reputation is great enough, and the purchaser is interested in reputations—and there are occasionally those who buy on reputation alone—the honorarium for a single portrait sometimes runs into several thousands. This is rare, however, and checks drawn for three figures, rather than four, are one's normal expectancy.

George Moore *by Edouard Manet. Courtesy, The Metropolitan Museum of Art, bequest of Mrs. H. O. Havemeyer, 1929. The H. O. Havemeyer Collection. The vitality of this painting depends, in part, on the jagged, nervous strokes which seem to be dashed in at great speed, with little concern for detail. The features are merely dabs of color, and the jacket is simply a mass of flat color, with a few light and dark strokes suggesting detail. The background, scrubbed in with casual diagonal strokes, leaves parts of the canvas exposed.*

Getting started

There are no rules for success. As in most professions, it is getting started that is the hardest. If you have aspirations in this field, you should first of all learn to do a commendable job (perhaps borrowing sitters to practice on), for obviously, unless you become a good painter, you will get nowhere.

When you have developed worthwhile skill, sooner or later someone will want to possess a portrait that you may have done solely for practice or fun. You may feel inclined to sell it at a ridiculously low price, or even to give it away. However commendable this intent may be, you should not yield to it—at least this is a wise general principle—for to do so might give you exactly the wrong start from a psychological standpoint. Remember, you have now become a capable artist. Your skill is rare. Few people have it. So your product has value. Think of it that way in your own mind and treat it that way! Establish a price which seems to you commensurate not only with the time and effort involved, but with your professional skill.

Of course, there is such a thing as setting your prices too high, frightening off all prospective customers. That could prove as disastrous as to charge too little. Plainly, it is better to get started at a reasonable figure than not to start at all. So perhaps you can discover a happy medium.

Whatever your compensation, taking a purely realistic view of the whole matter —which you really must do if you are to be a successful professional—the main thing, as I mentioned above, is not immediate income, but rather to exhibit your portraits as often as possible to build up interest in your work. In other words, do not hide your light under a basket.

If your work is truly good, and if enough people see it, your reputation will quickly grow, and soon commissions in increasing numbers will be coming your way. As the demand spreads, you may eventually be forced to raise your prices now and then in self-defense, because in painting portraits the nature of the work is such that you can do only so many each year.

Agents and galleries

Many artists are represented by agents, or sell through galleries where they exhibit their work, the agent or gallery receiving a percentage of sales. Now this is all very well for certain types of art work—landscapes or marines, for instance—but portraiture is a specialty in that the artist makes each painting to order. It is a definite commission, so his position is somewhat unique. When he is painting portraits he establishes a direct contact with his clients. Therefore, as a rule, commissions come directly to him, which means that generally he is not obliged to share his fee with a gallery or agent.

This does not indicate that there is any objection to galleries' or artists' agents. As a matter of fact, they make many an artist. *They* do not have to be modest, you see, so they are free to promote an artist's work and if they have the right contacts, they can do their promoting in important places. For example, they can often help to build an artist's reputation through publicity in the newspapers, art magazines, etc., assuming, of course, that the artist is a good painter. It is to their interest to set prices high and to raise them when they can, for their commission is a percentage of the selling price.

So the artist—especially the modest and retiring introvert who shuns business deals—may want to work through one or more selling agencies.

Many artists have what is perhaps the ideal arrangement in that they exhibit now and then and sell through some gallery or galleries without giving such agencies exclusive rights. In other words, they are free to accept commissions on their own. In any case, the average gallery is not much interested in a painter until his reputation is at least partly made, so he is generally on his own for a time. During this period, he can investigate the publicity and selling possibilities, if he so desires, deciding gradually what it is best to do.

Why paint portraits?

But if one enters into this work of painting portraits from a mercenary angle alone, he is quite certain to be disappointed. There *is* a living in it, as I have said, and rather a good living, providing—and that is a big word—one has the skill to do the work well, coupled with love of the work itself. Without that love, the work would be tiresome indeed, and little progress would be made. Love of one's work is really the artist's greatest and most lasting compensation.

PART TWO
Demonstrations by Professionals

Woman With a Towel, *Back View by Edgar Degas. Courtesy, The Metropolitan Museum of Art, bequest of Mrs. H. O. Havemeyer, 1929. The H. O. Havemeyer Collection. Toward the latter part of his life, Degas' work became increasingly broad and simplified. Masses of color were scribbled in with large, free, impatient strokes, and then just a few edges and details were defined with a dark stroke here and there. Notice how little detail this painting contains, except in the anatomy of the figure. The towel contains only a few distinct folds; the background is just a pattern of strokes; the hair and face are merely patches of color.*

Phase one. *The artist blocks in his composition in line, with only slight indications of the most significant dark areas. Note how the lines lightly begin, even at this early stage, to follow the direction of the forms over which they travel.*

15 / Albert Handell
Paints a Male Figure

Albert Handell is a New York artist whose work is shown at the ACA Gallery. In this painting, *Tony Seated*, the artist demonstrates his pastel techniques. Handell prefers to use a specially prepared pastel board rather than paper. It is also significant that he combines hard pastels with soft pastels. Here are the materials he uses and the reasons for his preferences.

Made by the F. Weber Company of Philadelphia, this particular pastel board is essentially a thick illustration board which is coated on one side with marble dust. The surface is something like extremely fine sandpaper. When the pastel stick is passed over the surface of the board, the granules of marble shave off the granules of color and hold them firmly to the board.

The artist tones the white ground of the pastel board with a thin, transparent wash of raw sienna gouache. This toned surface will show through all the colors the artist later applies, and will have a unifying effect, serving to integrate the lights, darks, and middle values.

Handell likes to use Nupastels for the initial blocking in of the forms. These are hard pastel sticks, manufactured by Eberhard Faber, which make a crisp line and are therefore extremely suitable for drawing. They are also good for adding accents in the later stages of the painting. The interplay of crisp lines and accents made by the hard pastels with the broad strokes of the soft pastels can be very effective.

It should be pointed out that Nupastels are rectangular, in contrast to the cylindrical form of soft pastels. Furthermore, hard pastels do not smudge quite so easily.

For most of the painting, Handell uses the traditional soft pastels, which are best for broad strokes and for large masses of color. The strokes of round pastels tend to be larger, bolder, and more ragged than the strokes of hard pastels. In a sense, soft pastels handle more like paint. He also has a preference for Grumbacher Tuffilm Spray No. 543, available in a pressure spray can.

Phase one: starting the painting

It is always advisable to have the model do something, rather than just sit there obviously posing for the picture. Here the artist selects a natural gesture instead of one of the stock poses of the art school studio model. This pose—the seated model leaning forward in his chair and grasping his right foot—gives the painting an air of liveliness, informality, and spontaneity.

After he has posed the model, the artist establishes his light source. To define form, simple lighting is always best. Simple lighting generally means one light source. The lighting coming from the side and slightly above (in this painting, from the upper right) has always been a popular choice with painters.

Handell begins his picture by drawing the figure with a hard pastel of burnt sienna. The warm tone of the burnt sienna harmonizes well with the wash of raw sienna which he previously used to tone the ground before painting. The burnt sienna also harmonizes with the flesh tones which will be applied over it at a later stage. The artist indicates the horizontals and verticals of the bed, wall, and chair; the diagonals of the torso, arms, legs, and feet; and the line of the waist. The fundamental composition of this painting is, in fact, based on the opposition of the geometric pattern of the chair and bed against the curves and diagonals of the figure itself. The static quality of the chair and bed also contrast with the active, dynamic quality of the figure.

Using the same crayon, the artist establishes some of the darks and middle values by means of diagonal strokes. Notice that even at this early stage, the direction of the strokes differs from the outline of the shapes the artist is drawing. For example, the strokes on the torso tend to follow the form *around*, as do the strokes on the shoulder. The strokes of the cast shadow on the floor give the illusion of lying flat. The strokes of the pastel, then, don't simply indicate the patterns of light and dark; they also suggest the form that the strokes are traveling over.

Darker areas are built up by hatching—which means by criss-crossing strokes. Note the placement of the figure and chair on the board. The artist has placed his figure a little off-center. He has also left a significant amount of space in the foreground, which will later purposely be left unfinished.

In phase one, then, Handell has firmly established the composition of his painting: he has decided where on the board to place the figure and chair; has indicated the over-all shape and gesture of the forms, as well as some of the darks and middle values; and has carefully observed and recorded the play of curved lines (head, shoulders, waist, right foot, chair arm) and straight lines (chair back, seat, left foot, background).

Phase two: further development of light and shade

The artist sprays his drawing with fixative and allows it to dry. He now switches to soft pastels, selecting sticks of burnt sienna, yellow ochre, gray-green, light blue-gray, red, black, and white. He begins to block in large areas of color—flesh tones, gray-green trousers, white towel, red chair seat, etc. He further develops the patterns of light, middle value, and dark, which are merely hinted at in phase one. Handell is careful to retain certain two dimensional shapes while he develops the volume of other forms in a three dimensional way. Having blocked in the flat tone of the trousers, for example, the artist goes back and adds a bit of modeling to re-establish the roundness of the form. The black patch of the chair behind the model's head is consciously kept flat and un-developed to stress its compositional value rather than its form. Notice, too, that the chair, towel, and bed are treated primarily as two-dimensional shapes, even though they do contain light and dark contrasts.

As he works, the artist begins to define the drawing more carefully. The head of the model has been enlarged, thrust forward, and moved left, closer to the shoulder. Hair and facial features, hands and feet emerge more definitely from the abstraction of the forms drawn in stage one. The chair and bed are given a clearer definition.

Phase two. *The basic colors of the figures are now blocked in very broadly with a minimum of detail. The first modeling appears on the arm and torso. The tones of the background are indicated, but not carried beyond a few rough strokes.*

125

Notice how Handell concentrates on his over-all value scheme to create the most effective possible pattern of lights, middle values, and darks. He has added a dark area in the upper right which throws the white of the bed into relief. The white towel now contrasts boldly with the middle and dark values of the flesh tones, chair, and trousers. These light value areas—towel and bed—flank the seated figure from behind and intensify the forward thrust of the body. The artist has developed the cast shadow on the floor with middle and dark values. This shadow, surrounding both chair and figure, at once anchors them to the floor and accentuates the diagonal thrust which begins with the arm of the chair, moves through the torso of the figure, and ends with the model's foot which is extended toward the lower right of the painting.

At this stage, the artist is still holding down detail, working instead with broad strokes on large areas. In fact, if you compare phase two with phase one, you will find that a certain amount of detail and a number of sharp edges have actually disappeared as the artist seeks to simplify his color areas. He will later put some details back in.

The artist is still careful of the pattern of the strokes. The strokes on the body still follow the form around; the strokes on the floor still seem to lie flat; the side of the chair is painted with vertical strokes following the direction of the chair. Notice how freely Handell scribbles in the diagonal strokes in the upper right hand section of the background. This ragged, unfinished quality will be retained in the final outer edges of the painting.

Phase three: development of color

At this stage, he blocks in the general tone of all the background areas. Even the areas left unfinished in the final picture, such as the upper right hand corner and the floor, are now developed a bit further. In the figure itself, the artist is beginning to add smaller, more precise details. Notice the modeling on the trousers which also enlivens the texture; note, too, the more detailed modeling on the arm, in which even the highlights are roughly indicated. Although details of the chair and some crisp edges are selectively added here and there, the chair is not carried as far as the figure. This selective finishing—which means carrying some parts of the painting into further detail than other parts—is an important feature of this painting. This method can be compared to selective focus in photography, in which some parts of the photograph are emphasized by being in sharp focus, while other parts are played down by being slightly out of focus.

Notice that the precise anatomical details of the arm, face, and feet are still roughly indicated as areas of tone and color. They will not be sharpened up until the final phase. The same is true of the folds in the towel and the details of the chair.

The artist, you will note, subordinates the background to the foreground. This technique serves to enhance the objects of principal interest. Although certain areas of any picture are always less important than others, their subordination should not disrupt the unity of the over-all composition. In this pastel, the artist successfully subordinates the background, yet preserves the unity of the picture in two ways: First, he uses a limited number of colors. Second, he crosshatches these few colors and develops an all over unity by the simple fact that his strokes literally interlock all over the painting. The average beginner, seeing the tremendous range of pastels available in art material stores, is inclined to feel he needs to own a number of them. Yet a wide variety of color

Phase three. *The forms are strengthened by the addition of darks, and contours are further defined, still without resorting to detail. The pattern of the background is established in various flat tones, roughly applied.*

effects can be realized with a very few pastel sticks if strokes of various colors are applied over one another so that they mix in the viewer's eye. Degas relied on this crosshatching technique to achieve the enormous richness of color in his pastels.

While working for richness of color, Handell also recognizes the importance of grays and neutrals, which offer the eye some rest and simultaneously accentuate the strong colors. This is one of the functions of a neutral background which is allowed to come through at various points of the painting. Here again, the technique of cross-hatching can produce these middle values. For example, if you take two strong colors and crosshatch them, they quiet each other down and produce subtle tones which would, by the way, turn muddy if you smudged them rather than crosshatched them.

Phase four: finishing the picture

The painting is once again sprayed with fixative and allowed to dry. Now the artist finally sharpens up the selected forms and adds detail wherever necessary. For example, he draws in all the fingers, but only the big toe; completes the modeling of the arm and torso, but just adds a few crisp lines to the chair and facial features, which give the impression of more detail than is actually there. The background areas are built up with additional broad strokes, but are left in rough form. Only one fold of the towel is sharply drawn; the others are just indicated.

Notice how selective Handell is about cast shadows. A strong cast shadow is indicated behind the foot to place it firmly on the floor and to direct the viewer's eye diagonally back into the picture. A strong cast shadow also defines the curve of the waist. The cast shadow on the towel, however, is merely hinted at so that the white shape is not interrupted by a large, intruding dark shadow.

The artist now puts in the final accents of color, taking care to keep the pastel fresh and bright to its completion. Notice how the warm over-all tone of the pastel board dominates all the colors and peeks through almost all the strokes. Even the cool strokes of the towel and bed mingle with the warmth of the background which comes through here and there. The blue trousers are not merely blue; they are laid over with warm strokes and also contain warm tones contributed by the exposed ground. In the same way, the artist reverses the process by placing strokes of cool color on the warm skin tones of the model—thus establishing a continuity of warm and cool color throughout the painting. Note that bright color has been used very spraringly—confined, in fact, to just two small areas of red on the chair.

Satisfied with his color accents, the artist once again sprays the painting with fixa-tive, then puts it aside. Returning to the picture after a week or two with a fresh eye, Handell now makes any small final corrections he thinks necessary. When these adjust-ments are complete, Handell selects two soft pastel sticks: one matches the dominant color of the painting; the other is its complementary color. Both colors are of the same value. In this case, the artist selects yellow-green and its complement, red-violet. With these pastels, he very lightly and gently adds almost invisible, feathery strokes of color over the entire painting, much as some artists put a final glaze over an oil painting.

After he has worked over the entire surface of the pastel in this way, Handell re-establishes accents of light and dark if need be. The pastel is given a final coat of fixative, immediately framed under glass, or covered with wax paper and stored flat.

Phase four. Tony Seated *by Albert Handell, 20″ x 20″. Collection, the Syracuse University Museum. Courtesy, AGA Gallery, New York. In the finished painting, the artist has been extremely selective in his use of detail and the degree of finish. The torso is carefully modeled, but the legs and chair are painted more flatly; the background remains an undetailed pattern of strokes; and much of the foreground is untouched.*

16/Albert Handell
Paints a Female Figure

Here Albert Handell demonstrates painting a female figure in pastels. In contrast to the preceding demonstration, this is a very relaxed, self-contained pose, in which the drama is achieved mainly by the lighting. This pastel painting is titled *Nude in Chair*.

For this demonstration, Handell again selects a combination of hard and soft pastels, and uses the same fixative as he did in the preceding painting. Instead of pastel board, however, the artist now chooses a heavy pastel paper of a neutral gray tone. Contributing its own cool tint, the gray paper will serve as a unifying undertone for the entire painting, in the same way as the raw sienna wash which toned the white ground in the previous demonstration.

Phase one: beginning the work

The artist again poses his model naturally, and positions her, relaxed with a book, in an overstuffed armchair. The light source is once again established at the upper right. It is usually wise to choose one dominant light source to reveal the forms most forcibly and most sharply.

With a hard pastel of burnt sienna, Handell quickly outlines the shapes of the objects which compose the painting, and he establishes the basic areas of dark, middle value, and light. Notice that the *light* values are not actually drawn in pastel, but are merely suggested at this stage by the untouched areas of the gray paper. The gray background, except for a few slight strokes to the left of the model's arm and above her head, is also left untouched.

Although the darks are indicated by crosshatching, it is interesting to note that the strokes are rarely crosshatched at right angles to each other (this would produce an unpleasant grid pattern). The strokes, more subtly laid on, tend to cross each other irregularly, and even to blend.

Notice how simple Handell's composition seems. The painting contains only three objects. Moreover, the three are treated as a single shape: chair, figure, and book are inseparably connected. But this simplicity is deceptive, for the artist is not concentrating on the objects themselves, but on volumes and shapes within them.

Literally every line in this painting curves. The rounded back of the chair curves around the model's head, flows down into the crooked elbow, swings around the arm of the chair, wiggles down to the corner, zigzags into the center, bends around the feet

---

Phase one. *Working in line, the artist develops the over-all rhythm of the pose, indicates the halftones and darks with light strokes, and establishes the direction which his strokes will follow in the final painting.*

into the cast shadow, turns back on itself and swings up again into the contours of the left arm of the chair, through the model's cylindrical arm, and back to the head. Notice the rounded forms of the lap and legs of the model, the roundness of her modeled knees. The artist has drawn strong curves at the hem of the skirt in the same way as he has treated the adjacent mound in the cusion. The head, again a rounded, egg-like shape, is topped by the mound of the hair, which is also visualized as a rounded form. The book, one of the few angular, flat forms in the painting, is actually a segment of an arc which swings from the model's uplifted arm down into the book, and up into the opposite elbow.

Notice once again how the strokes tend to follow the form. For example, the strokes on the book are parallel with the sides of the book; those on the arm tend to follow the arm around; the strokes on the right arm of the chair literally change direction as they follow the round shape of the chair. Even though these preliminary strokes will disappear by the time the pastel is finished, the artist has already established many of the directions his final strokes will follow.

Handell's composition is based on a balance of diagonals. The painting moves diagonally from the legs in the lower left, through the knees, torso, and jutting arm, into the back of the chair. The lines of the left chair arm, left shoulder, and head of the model also move diagonally from lower left to upper right.

To balance the composition, Handell has created a counter diagonal. Notice the thrust which begins at the model's right hand, and which pulls the viewer's eye diagonally down through the book into the model's lap, and down to the base of the chair on the lower right side of the painting.

In this initial phase, then, using only a hard pastel crayon, the artist has established his composition and indicated areas of light, middle value, and dark. By the pattern of his strokes, shading, and contouring, he has developed a very solid feeling of form throughout. The background has been left practically untouched. The chair is rendered abstractly. The figure, though heavily modeled, is still not drawn in detail. The artist has indicated brief touches of cast shadows beneath the model's feet and chair, placing them firmly on the ground. Cast shadows should always be used selectively and sparingly. Too many can destroy form. This is why the cast shadow of the foot is indicated by the fewest possible strokes.

Handell sprays his drawing with fixative and lets it dry before carrying it any further.

Phase two: introducing color into dark areas

Switching to soft pastels, the artist now develops the shadow areas and the darker patterns created by the skirt, chair, sandals, and book. He introduces red into the skirt, markedly subduing its warmth and intensity by crosshatching it heavily with burnt umber, and lightly with blue. The gray paper, showing through here and there, also helps cool the red. The deep shadow areas on the skirt are solidly stroked in with burnt umber and blue.

Phase two. *Working with broad strokes of soft pastel, Handell now blocks in his large tonal areas, keeping his shapes flat and his strokes open to allow the ground to shine through. He still does not apply pastel to the light areas; these are left untouched.*

The artist develops the book, laying thin parallel strokes one next to the other. The light areas of the flesh are not yet developed, but remain as they were in the drawing. The shadows on the model, however, are more strongly established in the legs, hands, shoulder, arm, neck, and face.

What was before a light shadow under the model's left foot now starts to become a sandal. The chair, though intentionally left rough and undetailed, is now attacked with broad, vigorous strokes that give it texture and solidity. Some red is introduced into the chair's back, arms, and cushion, but the intensity of the red is again modified with hatches and scribbles of burnt sienna. Touches of blue are added to the deep shadows on the arms and the base of the chair.

Look at the background. Notice how, with what appear to be the most random, stray lines, the artist has successfully suggested floor, walls, and even a corner.

Satisfied that he has carried the darks and shadowed areas as far as possible, Handell lightly sprays the work with fixative and proceeds to the next stage.

Phase three: developing lights and halftones

The artist now concentrates on rendering the light as he observes it falling on the model and chair, simplifying these light areas into patterns that contrast with the darker tones. The left side of the head, neck, chest, arms, hands, knees, and feet are strongly emphasized by light.

Handell begins to modify his shadow areas with darker accents such as the triangles of dark between the upper and lower arm of the model. He begins to develop halftones—areas midway between the light and the shadow—which the reader can see particularly on the model's face, neck, and legs. He also adds certain accents to define the form more clearly—the stroke of light along the top edge of the book and those along the top of the head, for example. The artist defines the knees and toes more clearly, but he still does not carry anything into great detail. The forms are still kept broad and general. Notice that a number of the halftones are actually achieved by the spaces between the light strokes, which allow the paper to come through and function as a halftone.

Once he has developed the lights and halftones to his satisfaction, the artist sprays the pastel with fixative and allows it to dry before he continues.

Phase four: flesh tones and details

It is significant that the artist does not use so-called "flesh" tones, although there are pastels available which are specially compounded to represent the various tones of flesh in light, halftone, and shadow. Handell recognizes that the color of flesh is not a standardized thing, but varies according to the effects of light and atmosphere. Thus he creates his own flesh tones by the use of unexpected colors which mix in the eye of the viewer.

Phase three. *Now the artist begins to block in his lights, interlacing them with his halftones and allowing the middle tones of the ground to show below his light strokes. Note that the details of the face and hands are still not defined.*

The luminous flesh tones on the body of the model appear to be composed of dozens of colors which shimmer with light. This luminosity is actually created mainly with delicate pink, blue, dusty yellow, and dusty brown. These colors are either juxtaposed (strokes of different colors laid side by side) or crosshatched (strokes of different colors crossed one over the other). Juxtaposing intensifies the colors and makes them vibrate in the eye of the viewer. Crosshatching, like mixing oil paints on the palette, allows the artist to create secondary and tertiary colors.

The hair and the light falling on the right shoulder, arm, and hand are rendered in broad strokes of soft yellow. Yellow is stroked over the entire body, hatched and juxtaposed with blue to make various tones of green, and with red to make tones of pinkish-orange. The red and blue work together to produce the cool tones on the body, ranging from dusty red, to pink, to shades of lavender.

To render the light falling on the cool red chair, the artist again uses his yellow crayon to create warm notes of orange. The color of the floor is faintly indicated with strokes of orange. White is used sparingly—above the eyebrow, on the collarbone, and on the knob of the knees, etc.—to emphasize highlights and to give a pearly glow to the flesh.

In this final stage, Handell gives his painting the finishing touches, adding facial features and other details. Notice the dark hollows he has added to the ears and eyes. These details are still kept slightly out of focus so that one does not, for example, see actual eyelashes, eyebrows, etc. The artist also adds crisp, dark strokes to define more precisely the anatomical contours of the model's left arm, the shape of the legs, and the finger of her left hand.

Details, however, are used very selectively. The model's left hand, for example, has only one finger clearly defined. The other fingers blend into the shadow as a single shape. In the same way, he draws the toes of one foot more precisely than he draws the toes of the other. Handell means to suggest more detail than is really there.

The artist now sprays his pastel with fixative and puts it aside for a time. After a week or two, he returns to his painting and now concentrates on the final harmonizing of colors. Using blue and neutral gray pastel sticks, Handell lightly strokes over the entire painting—in the same way as he did in the previous demonstration—to give it a slightly cooler tonality. He now gives the completed pastel painting a final coat of fixative.

Phase four: Nude in Chair *by Albert Handell, 25½" x 19½". Collection, Mr. & Mrs. Gerald Rosenberg. Courtesy, ACA Gallery, New York. In the final phase, Handell introduces a few crisp strokes to define edges, facial features, and some of the fingers. Although the figure has been carried to a relatively finished state, many contours still remain elusive, and the chair is a pattern of strokes rather than a precise form.*

17/Harvey Dinnerstein
Paints a Nude

Harvey Dinnerstein is a noted American painter who works in a variety of media in addition to pastel. His work may be seen at the Kenmore Galleries in Philadelphia.

Dinnerstein, who notes that pastel has been misjudged in recent times as a lightweight, frivolous medium limited to expressing pretty or ephemeral subjects, is himself impressed by its flexibility and adaptability to many subjects, moods, techniques, and effects. He believes—and his work substantiates—that pastel is a completely realized medium quite as substantial and powerful as any other.

Phase one: drawing in charcoal

Here Harvey Dinnerstein demonstrates his technical approach to pastel as he paints this work, *Nude With Towel*. The classical pose of a seated nude woman drying her feet was suggested to him by Greek sculpture, which has long interested him and which has sometimes served as a point of departure for his own work. His intent was to capture the classical feeling of movement in the body, yet to avoid the sterility of an idealized, academic painting. Using the classical pose as a springboard, Dinnerstein wanted to work toward achieving a contemporary, flesh and blood female, caught in a moment of quiet intimacy.

The artist begins by selecting a prepared pastel canvas, manufactured by Grumbacher, which he tones with a transparent wash of raw umber (those experienced with the medium concur that the vibrancy and brilliance of pastels diminish against a white background). The tinted ground, which influences each stroke of color, gives immediate unity and luminosity to the surface of the canvas. Because the ground will play an important part in the painting, acting as a middle value against which the lights and darks will be adjusted, and influencing the total color harmony of the work, Dinnerstein must begin with quite a definite idea of the colors he intends to use over this ground.

After the umber wash has dried, Dinnerstein begins to work with charcoal. At this stage he blocks in his forms and begins to establish his values. He works very quickly and broadly, concentrating on the over-all composition. As he outlines the figure, notice how he focuses on breaking up the large shapes into patterns of light (leg, arms, chest, left shoulder), halftone (torso, thigh, face, right shoulder), and dark (head and

Phase one. *The artist begins by blocking in the large shapes in charcoal. The emphasis is on the over-all distribution and value of the compositional elements, rather than on contour or detail. In a sense, this first stage is an abstraction in black and white.*

hair); he is not yet concerned with achieving anatomical fidelity. The towel, arms, and leg are treated as one abstract shape. What the viewer's eye accepts as the model's left arm and side is nothing more than an elongated triangle, indicated as a middle value. Although this preliminary charcoal stage is called a "drawing," line is actually used very sparingly—to show, for example, the contour which begins at the back of the model's head and follows through her neck, shoulder, back, and hip. The artist is much more interested in searching for correct value relationships than he is in modeling the forms.

Notice how decisively and boldly Dinnerstein places his darks—in the upper right background, beneath the bent leg, in the head, and at various points beneath and to the right of the figure. These are vigorously applied in broad, painterly strokes.

The umber ground momentarily suffices to indicate the lightest values in the towel and figure. The artist now lightly sprays the charcoal drawing with fixative and turns to pastel.

Phase two: developing the drawing in pastel

Dinnerstein generally works with soft pastels which he likes for their rich, meaty surface, though at times he uses Talens semi-soft pastels. He tends to wield his chalks like a paint brush, breaking the pastel sticks into stumpy pieces, and using their wide, flat surfaces for broad areas, while relying on the edges of the stumps to render details.

Although Dinnerstein has a large collection of pastels in many hues, he chooses a limited number of colors for any one painting, selecting them as he goes along and keeping them in his hand as he paints. He works with two hues of the same value—one warm, one cool—using them interchangeably one on top of another, and stroking back and forth until he achieves a vibration of light and color within the form. Because pastel is a direct medium—that is, colors are mixed directly on the support rather than on the palette—Dinnerstein selects more intense colors than he would normally use in another medium, and from them creates an endless variety of subtle tones on the surface of the painting.

Dinnerstein, who works from dark to light, characterizes pastel as essentially a scumbling medium. Scumbling means applying an opaque or semi-opaque layer of paint over a ground color to cover the underlying layer partially or fully. Like impasto, the technique of scumbling builds up the thickness of the paint surface, giving it dimension and a sculptural quality. Dinnerstein, who adapts this technique to the medium of pastel, scumbles lighter colors semi-transparently over darker ones.

In this stage of the painting, the artist defines and develops his forms in pastel. Working from the model, but only using her as a point of departure, he strives to achieve a subtle balance between particularization and generalization or, if you will, between realism and abstraction. For example, he pays closer attention to the anatomy of the figure and works toward a clearer definition. This clarification, evident through-

Phase two. *Dinnerstein develops tonal relationships by stroking in his lights and developing his darks, still without refining contours or adding details. The strokes on the figure now begin to follow the form; notice the horizontal on the upper arms, and the vertical strokes on the forearms and the lower leg. The rough texture of the background now begins to emerge, and the white impasto of the towel is applied.*

out the figure in the arms, head, hair, and torso, is particularly striking in the bent leg which offers the artist a challenging problem of foreshortening. On the other hand, the back of the chair, the drapery on which the model is seated, and the towel are developed very generally—that is, the forms are suggested rather than rendered naturalistically.

The artist focuses on consolidating his formal structure, emphasizing the rising and falling, step-like patterns of the towel, body, and back of the chair. The towel, now the lightest value in the painting, is heavily modeled to give it weight and substance. The colors, in places where the strokes actually disappear, look as though they'd been *painted* on with a palette knife, rather than stroked on with a stick of pastel. Dinnerstein achieves this impasto effect by applying color, thickly spraying it with fixative, then applying another layer of color over the same area. The texture apparent in the contrasting, lightly worked areas of the towel is the result of the rough weave of the canvas showing through, rather than the effect of the pastel strokes themselves.

At one point when Dinnerstein felt the towel was becoming too dense, he sprayed it with a fixative to lower the value, then worked back over it to increase the sense of light and volume by developing the opaque, buttery, paint-like qualities in certain areas, and contrasting them with the more airy and transparent shadows of the folds.

Dinnerstein will often use fixative to alter or modify the direction of his work. If, for example, an area is going dead, he will spray it with fixative, then strike back into it with pastels to revive the intensity and freshness of the color. He uses the same technique to warm or cool an area. At one point, for instance, the background area around the head became too hot. Dinnerstein applied fixative to lower the value, then worked back into the passage with a cool, grayish raw umber. When the shadow areas in the drapery and foreground became too dark and dense, he again used fixative, then worked back into them with a warm blue-gray to heighten the luminosity.

While the tones in phase one were simply indicated by rough blurs of charcoal, with little emphasis on distinct strokes, now the strokes of pastel begin to follow the contours of the shapes. Notice particularly how the horizontal and vertical strokes on the figure tend to follow the contours of the limbs and torso. The interlacing of light and dark strokes which characterizes the flesh tones of the final picture also begins to take shape here. The face is still seen merely as a silhouette, with no indication of eyes, nostrils, or lips. The tones of the background are still thinly applied as compared to the heavier applications of color in the figure. This difference in handling will remain in the final phase.

Notice the intense contrasts between the lights, halftones, and darks. They will later be modified, but at the moment they help differentiate the planes (foreground, middleground, background) and clarify the source of light, and its effect, as it travels from the upper right corner and falls on the objects. The intermediate stage is lightly sprayed with fixative and allowed to dry.

Phase three: refining the pastel

Dinnerstein now proceeds to refine the color harmony and forms of the painting, and, for the first time, he adds details. He defines the facial features, hand, and fingers. He identifies the light source on the viewer's right as a window veiled by a transparent curtain which softens and diffuses the light, and which gives a feeling of space and air.

The back of the chair, which has been developed very generally with a cool blue-green, scumbled semi-transparently over the umber ground, has now become quite intense. That one small passage of bright color, added to the otherwise muted palette, has several important effects. The blue-green helps define the sense of distance between the figure and the wall and window behind her. The shape and color of the blue-green (the light value makes it advance visually) accentuate the curve and forward thrust of the model. And this passage skillfully adds visual excitement to the subtle, subdued color scheme.

Notice that in spite of its intensity, this blue-green area does not intrude on or disrupt the over-all harmony of the painting. On the contrary, the bright color area enhances the color scheme. The flesh tones in the figure, as already mentioned, are built from a balance between cool light green earth and warm brown. In the same way, this bright cool area of bluish-green relates to and balances with the warm scumbled ochre of the window and drapery.

It is interesting to note that the strokes on the drapery in the chair tend to be vertical, even though the forms are themselves diagonal. These vertical strokes give a more architectural feeling to the drapery and are less likely to detract attention from the figure. It is also interesting to see how the strokes in the background take advantage of the texture of the canvas. In contrast to the decisive strokes on the figure, the background strokes are applied very thinly and merely skim over the ridges of the canvas.

Notice how the artist has now modified the dramatic value contrasts so apparent in the previous stage. The transitions from light to halftone to dark are softer and smoother—more suited to the pervasive mood of quiet intimacy and to the tones of diffused light. The cool yellow towel is toned down; the gray-black drapery is lightened; the modeling and shadows on the figure are more delicate. To achieve this softer effect, the artist has stroked middle tones over the background which darken the originally light strokes and which lighten the originally dark strokes. He has used the same technique to soften the contrast in the drapery on which the model sits. This modification between light and dark in the drapery has the added effect of focusing the viewer's attention on the figure. The artist has continued to interlace strokes of light and shade on the figure, building up a network of very delicate tones. The edges of the figure are more clearly defined, but with a minimum of reliance on line. Notice how some edges—like the line of the back—are crisp, while others—like the upper arm nearest the viewer—are soft and melting. In contrast to the preceding phase, the edges of the blue drapery have actually been softened by blurring the tone into some parts of the background area.

The artist continues to make final adjustments until he is satisfied with the total harmony of the painting. Although he uses fixative during the development of his work to seal off one stage from another and to obtain special effects, Dinnerstein does not like to risk the likelihood of fixative disturbing his final color harmony. Rather than apply a final coat of fixative to his now completed pastel painting, the artist prefers to protect its surface by covering it with paper or glass.

Detail of Nude with Towel *by Harvey Dinnerstein.*

Phase three: Nude with Towel *by Harvey Dinnerstein. 15½″ x 11½″. Collection,ᵒ Mr. & Mrs. Bernard Bless. Courtesy, Kenmore Galleries, Philadelphia. In the final painting, the contours of the figure are carried to completion; details of the hands and face are added; and dark notes are cautiously placed to define edges here and there. As a foil for the relative precision of the figure, the towel remains rough, and the background is still handled in an abstract way. Note how little detail there is in the drapery on the chair, and in other background elements.*

Phase one. *This charcoal drawing, along with small thumbnail color sketches, was done on location and then brought to the studio to form the basis of the final painting. The preliminary drawing establishes the placement of the various elements in space—the darks looking up in the foreground and the grayer shapes receding into the atmosphere.*

18/Harvey Dinnerstein Paints a Landscape

In the step-by-step construction of this work, titled *Morning Smog*, Harvey Dinnerstein exploits the advantages of pastel as a medium for landscape painting. Pastel—particularly suited for landscape work because of its ability to quickly capture the delicate, ephemeral nuances of atmosphere and light—allows the artist to work directly, rapidly, immediately, and without interruption.

To get the maximum benefit from these inherent advantages, however, requires careful planning, for one must be ready at any given moment to take down on paper or canvas a mood of light and air that can evaporate as quickly as it appears. Therefore, it is simply not realistic to think of taking all your materials with you on location—canvas, board, pastel paper, sketchbook, charcoal, watercolor or gouache and brushes to apply your ground, fixative, and a vast selection of pastels—and then decide on the spot which to actually use. Equipment must be pared down to the essentials, and, wherever possible, prepared in advance.

Dinnerstein—who frequently limits his location work to making color notations and charcoal drawings, which he takes back to the studio where he undertakes the final painting—carries a minimum of materials on location: a sketch pad and charcoal, a basic set of Talens semi-soft pastels (they are less cumbersome than soft pastels), and a rough surface pastel board which he often tints in advance with one or more tones for making quick color notations on a small scale. Thus prepared for all possibilities, Dinnerstein may occasionally do a few studies on one sheet.

Such careful elimination and preparation permits Dinnerstein to record instantly, without preliminary setting up, any passing phenomenon which catches his eye. Moreover, instead of making notes at random, he generally focusses his energies on observing; he scouts around until he is struck by a visual idea. In comparison to this lengthy period of observation, the amount of time he actually spends working on his notes is minimal.

Phase one: working on location

The idea for *Morning Smog* came to Dinnerstein quite unexpectedly. Driving along the New Jersey Turnpike, one foggy morning, shortly after his return to the States from a year of painting and study in Rome, his eye caught the back view of the Statue of Liberty. The unexpected view of the familiar symbol, seen in the morning fog beyond the decayed pilings, evoked an immediate response. He determined to return at his first opportunity.

Dinnerstein went back to the site and, following his usual procedure, made many small pastel color notations of the view at different times of day and under different conditions of light and atmosphere. His color notations are made very quickly, with no attention to detail. He works small for the sake of time and convenience, noting what he sees in terms of color and balance, recording changing moods and lighting conditions, and testing total color relationships. These notations—which are always a record of the whole picture, rather than separate studies of each of its parts—visualize the artist's direct and immediate response to nature in terms of light, air, and form.

After he has finished his color notations, the artist makes one or more charcoal sketches of the subject. He works larger than he did in the color notations in order to study the subject in greater detail and to give the silhouette of the statue more definition. With the point of the charcoal, he crisply outlines the silhouette, placing it almost exactly in the center of the paper.

He then blocks in the foreground. By adding the dark, broad, emphatic pilings in the lower left of the foreground, Dinnerstein skillfully changes the perspective of the statue, a shift which immediately gives visual excitement to the entire composition. Now the viewer's eye is drawn first to the pilings, then led diagonally across the drawing from the lower left to the statue. The viewer has the impression of looking at the statue from an angle. If you shield the pilings with your hand, you will notice that you automatically confront the statue head on. Still holding your hand over the pilings, notice how unexciting the composition has become.

In this preliminary drawing, the artist carefully records the separation of planes to create a feeling of space and distance between the foreground, middle distance, and background. Following the principle that the intensity of colors diminishes as they grow more distant, Dinnerstein places his darkest dark in the left foreground where the viewer's eye enters the painting, then graduates the tones from dark to halftone to light according to their size and distance from this point. The light horizontal band indicated on the right between the statue and the foreground is water. The horizon is placed with a light gray at the base of the right side of the statue.

Several color studies and one charcoal drawing are all Dinnerstein did outdoors. He took these notes back to his studio, where he painted the final landscape. Although, from time to time, he still completes a work on the spot, Dinnerstein has gradually shifted away from depending too much on naturalistic phenomena, and has tended over the years to finalize landscape work in his studio.

Phase two: planning the painting

In this painting, and in his work in general, Dinnerstein tries to establish a subtle balance between the poles of naturalism (the precise, photographic duplication of nature) and of arbitrarily imposed stylization—what he calls "meaningless mannerism."

What Dinnerstein works toward, and what he believes most successfully suggests life, is a reordering and a distilling of the essential qualities of nature, interpreted in the light of human experience. This quest involves a merciless, discriminating selectivity at each moment of painting; of answering and re-answering the question, "Is this pictorial element essential or extraneous to the central purpose of this work?"

To illustrate his point, Dinnerstein refers to the works of other artists which embody these concepts. He singles out the landscapes and seascapes of the American

Phase two. *Without making any attempt to render edges or detail, the artist broadly blocks in the placement of his various tones, and establishes the rough texture which will characterize the finished painting. He has not yet made a precise division of his planes into foreground, middle ground, and background, but has concentrated on the distribution of shapes.*

painter Albert Pinkham Ryder which project a powerful emotional quality that has nothing whatever to do with the naturalistic description of leaves, sky, moon, or sea.

Dinnerstein also admires the work of Alfred Meryon, a French artist whose etchings of nineteenth century Paris offer an incisive psychological statement about life in the city. Dinnerstein recalls one etching, a rather ghoulish work titled *The Morgue*, which records an incident of a corpse being fished from the Seine. Although the figures and the activity in which they are engaged are presumably the subjects of this work, they are quite small—almost incidental to the buildings rising behind them. It is the architecture, not the figures themselves, which express the tragedy. This ability to infuse objects with life and to make them express the human condition is the compelling quality Dinnerstein discovers in the best works of the twentieth century American painter Edward Hopper.

It is within the frame of reference of Ryder, Meryon, and Hopper that Harvey Dinnerstein approaches his pastel landscape.

In examining and arranging his color notations, Dinnerstein realized that none captured the particular quality which he had observed from his automobile window, and which was still fresh in his memory. The conditions of light and atmosphere had changed so irrevocably that the image etched in his memory did not exist, in fact, when he returned to the site. Since the color notes spread before him were useless, he decided to discard them and work exclusively from the charcoal sketch and from memory. Once this decision was made, Dinnerstein arranged his pastels and prepared his panel.

Phase three: starting the painting

Although pastel panels are commercially available, Dinnerstein prefers to make his own. To do this, he selects a quality, heavy weight, 100% rag board and prepares the surface as follows. First he mixes ground pumice (marble dust and silicone are also suitable) into a gesso solution, varying the amount of pumice according to the texture he wishes to obtain. The greater the amount of pumice, the grainier the surface of the paper. He then applies this gesso-pumice solution to the paper with a brush or palette knife. Dinnerstein finds that the knife builds up the textured ground less mechanically than the brush.

The gesso, which dries almost immediately, is now tinted with a transparent wash of watercolor. Dinnerstein decided to use green earth as a ground to complement the sulphurous tonality of the color scheme he had in mind. When the wash was dry, he blocked in the broad masses with charcoal: the pilings in the foreground; the horizontal band in the middle distance on which the statue rests; the statue itself; the mist and smoke that swirls from the right side of the statue toward the upper right hand corner; and the sliver of land suggested on the horizon. He established all these forms in a uniform gray, a lower middle value.

The artist then blocked in the sky and water over the green wash, using gray, Naples yellow, and, for the sky, a light red earth. He stroked warm umber and black over the pilings in the foreground to bring them forward. He used a bluish-gray to make the pilings in front of the statue recede; green-gray and light red earth intermixed to make the statue recede; and light blue and light red to make the last plane of the landscape recede.

Phase three. *Now the artist begins to divide his subject into foreground, middle ground, and background planes. The strong darks at the lower left loom close to the spectator, while the statue recedes into the distance, yet obviously stands nearer the viewer than the murky sky. On two separate planes are the pilings in the middle ground and the distant shore, each defined by a value which differs slightly from the other planes.*

Phase four: completing the painting

Since this landscape painting depends entirely on suggestion for its impact, completing it was not a question of moving from the general to the specific, of defining forms and adding details. Rather, it involved reducing a powerful symbol—one already highly charged with emotion—to its physical essentials, and then placing it in an atmosphere or context which expressed the artist's personal reaction to that universal symbol.

To achieve the effect he sought, Dinnerstein relied heavily—almost exclusively, in fact—on a subtle, masterful use of color. To suggest the haze of rising sun behind the fog, Dinnerstein chose a light red, which he first concentrated in one spot and then melted into the blue-gray area to the left and right of the sun. He delicately used the same red to suggest the sun's reflection on the water.

At first dissatisfied with the red (its value was too high, its hue too sweet for the subject and mood), Dinnerstein began to work over it to create the smoky, grayish-pink which appears in the final state. He repeatedly sprayed the area with fixative to lower the value. This technique, which may be compared to glazing in oil painting procedures, was used throughout the painting to modify the color scheme. For example, Dinnerstein built up the sky and its reflection on the water with ochre, Naples yellow, and light green earth, continually glazing with fixative to lower the values and to contribute a special quality of mystery to the atmosphere. He particularly depended on glazing to establish the pattern of the smoke which drifts from the statue to the upper right hand corner.

Fixative is a liquid. If used heavily enough, it will actually dissolve the chalk in which the ground pigments are suspended, and thereby modify the final color. Moreover, fixative can also change a shape, albeit quite subtly. If you compare stages two and three, you will see that Dinnerstein's use of fixative actually altered the original shape of the pattern of smoke—in the very way the artist intended.

If you again compare this stage of the painting with its predecessor, you will notice that the values have been adjusted to develop a more precise idea of the placement in space of various pictorial ideas. For instance, the dark clouds in the remotest distance have been lightened in order to force the statue a bit forward. Moreover, the pilings immediately in front of the island have been darkened in order to establish the placement of the sky. Finally, the immediate foreground has been located by the decisive dark of the pilings in the left foreground. The artist has also lightened the sky behind the upper portion of the statue, and refined the outline of the statue to make it stand out more clearly.

The pumice, locked into the gesso ground, contributes its own interesting texture and helps bring out the mottled quality of the sky. The sense of mystery and turbulence in the sky is created less by the strokes of the pastel than by the effect of the pumice-gesso mixture which imposes itself on the chalk as it moves across the rough surface.

The pumice-gesso ground serves a second, equally important function. Because of its toothiness, it can grab and hold greater quantities of chalk than a smoother working surface would permit. This toothiness enabled the artist to build up, glaze, and work back into his painting until all the rawness of color had disappeared and he had re-created the fleeting moment between light and dark, and the equally ephemeral nuances between mistiness and clarity which the artist had remembered seeing.

Phase four: Morning Smog *by Harvey Dinnerstein, 10″ x 15½″. Collection of the artist. Courtesy, Kenmore Galleries, Philadelphia. Although the final painting still emphasizes silhouette rather than detail, contours are slightly sharpened—though they are still relatively soft throughout the painting. The subtle decisions regarding which contours should be sharpened and which should remain soft are similar to selective focus, which is an important compositional device in photography.*

Phase one. *The artist lightly draws in his composition in charcoal. The purpose of this drawing is simply to establish the placement of the elements, rather than to render detail, since this drawing will disappear beneath the underpainting which follows.*

19 / Aaron Shikler
Paints a Portrait

Aaron Shikler is a versatile painter who works with equal skill in oil and pastel. The artist's work may be seen at the Davis Galleries, New York. His pastels are celebrated for their unorthodox effects which are generally regarded as beyond what the medium can normally accomplish. By frequently breaking the "rules," Shikler achieves a range of light and color effects which amply demonstrate that pastel is a full-fledged painting medium that can rival oil for subtlety and finish.

Shikler finds pastel a challenge to his technical proficiency and creative ingenuity. Like Edgar Degas before him, he has confronted the restrictions of pastel and has developed a number of unusual techniques to break through these limitations. The frequently unconventional procedures apparent during this demonstration, *Woman With Guitar*, reflect a fresh approach to pastel and produce subtle, rather than flamboyant results. His methods are ways of extracting the latent potential of pastel, and are not displays or tricks meant to impress the viewer or to disguise the true qualities of pastel and masquerade it as another medium.

Phase one: the charcoal sketch

Paint, whether it is oil, watercolor, tempera, or acrylic, is composed of ground pigments suspended in a liquid. In pastel, the pigments are suspended in a liquid substance called gum tragacanth which, when it dries, takes on the characteristics of chalk. This chalk-pigment combination produces an airy, luminous effect which sets it apart from any other paint medium. On the other hand, oil, watercolor, gouache, acrylic, and other opaque paints—because they are liquids—can be built up, layer upon layer, almost indefinitely. This characteristic, which permits the artist great freedom to explore and change as he works, is not found in the "dry" medium of pastel.

There is a point past which paper, canvas, or board simply cannot hold any more pigmented chalk. At this point the artist experiences the frustrating phenomenon of being, in Shikler's words, "locked out," that is, unable to proceed any further because of the physical limitations of pastel.

The locking out point *cannot* be indefinitely circumvented. It can, however, be postponed. One way to do this is by choosing an appropriate support for the type of pastel you intend to undertake. Shikler, for example, rarely uses pastel paper because no matter how rough the texture, paper cannot hold enough chalk for his purposes. Canvas prepared with glue size, on the other hand, has a gritty texture which "grabs" the pastel and makes it adhere. For even more holding power, Shikler relies on pastel

Phase two. *A casein underpainting is now freely brushed in. The colors are muted versions of the pastel hues which will be applied after the underpainting has dried. The advantage of this casein underpainting is that broad color areas are blocked in without building up a layer of pastel—for once the artist begins to apply pastel, there is an inherent limit to the number of layers he can apply, and therefore a limit to the number of changes he can make.*

board, a hardboard with fine quality, rag paper glued over it and covered with marble dust or silicone. Its fine sandpaper surface holds the greatest amount of pastel.

For this demonstration, the artist selected a pastel board which he toned with a transparent wash of casein. This toning procedure, similar to a technique favored by the old masters, allows the white of the board to show through the wash, contributing a luminous quality to the paint surface. When he applies the wash, Shikler already has a color scheme in mind, for the tone he selects must harmonize with the colors which will go over it. In this case, the artist selected a fawn gray.

After the wash dries, Shikler begins to sketch in his subject with a soft, rich charcoal. He establishes his composition, here basing it on a simple pyramid built from the shapes of the woman and the guitar. The charcoal sketch simply places the figure on the canvas in the most minimal way. When the sketch is complete, Shikler lightly fixes it with charcoal fixative and allows it to dry.

Shikler is quite particular about the kind of fixative he uses. He avoids the commercial types sold in spray cans, finding such synthetic-based fixatives viscous, prone to shininess, and difficult to control. He much prefers traditional pastel fixative, a 2% varnish, 98% alcohol mixture, which he uses in conjunction with a good mouth atomizer —a type of applicator which he believes offers the artist the greatest degree of control.

Phase two: the casein underpainting

After the charcoal sketch is completed, Shikler begins the second stage of his work. Rather than going directly into pastel, however, he now works in casein. With a rough bristle brush and a generous amount of water, he builds up over his sketch with very thin casein colors. Keeping his palette gray in tone, he selects subdued versions of the pastel colors which will go over the casein, and broadly blocks in the figure, guitar, and background in neutral tones of reds, yellows, olive greens, and orange. Although the artist does begin to work on the background, he is not yet interested in building up texture, but is merely experimenting in color, searching out proper values to bring the drawing together.

A certain heaviness and roughness are apparent in the intermediary casein stage. This very broad quality contrasts noticeably with the delicacy of the charcoal drawing and the fineness of the finished pastel. Like a stage in the construction of a building, the casein underpainting is not intended to be "pretty." Its purpose is structural, for it serves as the unadorned support on which the succeeding pastel layers will rest. Some of the casein underpainting will show through here and there, contributing to an airy, exciting surface. Most important, casein enables Shikler to work out all the problems of composition and color freely, without building up a layer of pastel. Underpainting in casein, in short, is an extremely important technique in helping the artist postpone the "locking out" point previously mentioned.

Phase three: the pastel

When the casein underpainting has dried, Shikler begins to work in soft pastels. He keeps a large, complete set of pastels to work from, arranged as they are purchased

Phase three. *Shikler now applies pastel to his casein underpainting, stroking chalk lightly over the casein which shines through and unifies the over-all color effect. Note the precise strokes of the face, in contrast to the seemingly random (but really controlled) strokes on the dress. Certain contours are sharpened with charcoal, but precise drawing is saved for the final stage.*

158

in their own case. As the pastels break or wear down, he places the chips in small metal cigar boxes, according to their tone. All colors of related tones are placed in one box. These pieces are used for adding details.

Shikler imposes no restrictions on the number of colors he uses in any one painting. He may work with many or few, as judgment dictates. However, he works with only one color at a time, placing it all over the painting—wherever he thinks it should go—before he switches to another color. This technique, he feels, greatly helps him retain color balance at all times.

To heighten the excitement and intensity of his work, Shikler generally uses complementary colors of the same value, pairing, for example, related tones of red and green, yellow and purple, etc. He also exploits the tendency of complementary colors to intensify each other when placed side by side in yet another way. If an area is going dead, he will revive it by lightly stroking a neutralizer, such as pale umber, around the area. By surrounding the colors with a grayish tone, he makes an otherwise dull area appear more intense.

If, on the other hand, an area is too harshly colored, Shikler will tone it down by blending or will make adjacent areas appear more vibrant by lightly feathering the offending surface with soft charcoal. The area will be subdued, but will still retain its freshness of color. To create shadows or to suggest depth, he will again feather with charcoal, but more heavily.

To blend, modify, or darken areas without applying darker tones of pastel or feathering with charcoal, Shikler relies on fixative. An area toned down with fixative can be left as it is or reworked with additional layers of pastel.

The artist uses fixative both in orthodox and unorthodox ways. Like most pastellists, he fixes each stage of his work to seal it off from the next; moreover, he will fix any individual area which satisfies him and which he wants to protect from change. For more substantial, painterly effects than pastel ordinarily produces, Shikler relies on two techniques. He will build up the surface by alternately stroking with his pastels and spraying with fixative. Or he will dip his chalk directly into a bottle of fixative and then stroke the wet pastel directly onto the surface of the painting. The second technique, startling though it may sound, actually permits him to control impasto effects more closely than the alternate pastel-fixative approach. The effect is also somewhat more dense.

Notice the many different textures in this painting: hair, flesh, quilted brocade, wood, tortoise shell, and metal are all readily described and developed within the boundaries of pastel by Shikler's expert manipulation. To define and emphasize the fall of the woman's hair, his pastel strokes follow, for example, the direction of the hair itself. The flesh tones and textures are developed by sensitive use of color and by sophisticated stroking.

Green earth is the basis of the skin tones in this pastel—as in all Shikler's paintings. Working from dark to light, the artist begins with green earth, then slowly builds up into the lights first with burnt or raw umber halftones, and then with Naples yellow. For maximum reality, Shikler adds final highpoints of cadmium reds and earth reds to the cheeks, elbows, ears, knuckles, tip of the nose, and lips. To blend and ease too broad a stroke on the flesh, or to soften crosshatched strokes without obliterating them, Shikler uses a traditional stump, a soft paper rolled into a stick.

Phase four: Woman with Guitar *by Aaron Shikler, 24″ x 30″. Collection, Mr. & Mrs. William Y. Dear, Jr. Courtesy, Davis Galleries, New York. In the final phase, layer upon layer of pastel strokes are built up to develop precise modeling in the forms of the face, limbs, and instrument, while freer strokes and rougher textures are retained in the dress and background. Notice how the background subtly reflects the warm and cool tones that appear in the figure.*

To capture the rich highlights and heaviness of the quilted satin robe, Shikler attacks the canvas vigorously and boldly, scribbling, stippling, crosshatching, and juxtaposing his strokes as his intuition and experience direct him. Cadmium yellow, chrome yellow, olive green, and cadmium orange retain their purity in some spots, mingle in others. Pastels are applied dry, then sprayed with fixative, or dipped directly into the fixative and applied wet. The shadows and deep folds which contribute to the feeling of weight in the fabric and which emphasize the pyramidal shape of the skirt falling from the knees, are rendered in burnt sienna, deep ochres, and deep olive greens. The sleeves are built from cadmium red, pale red, burnt sienna, and touches of charcoal. To heighten the effect of red, opposing, that is complementary, greens are used.

Using a tighter, more precise technique, Shikler develops textures of wood, tortoise shell, and metal in the guitar. The greens and browns in the curved body of the instrument are carefully juxtaposed and lightly blended to create a smooth, grained, polished surface. The pastels in the darker neck of the guitar are so densely applied and carefully blended that individual strokes cannot be seen. The mottled tortoise shell guard on which the woman's hand rests is developed by precise stippling, while the hard, cold quality of metal in the tuning pegs and frets is created with daubs of blue and gray pastel, discriminatingly applied. Charcoal crisply outlines the shape of the guitar, as well as the edge of the model's arms and her right shoulder.

Notice that the background is built up from subdued tones of the same colors which compose the figure and the guitar: earth red, olive green, and umber, which acts as a neutralizer. The over-all effect is soft, in contrast to the dazzling robe, yet subtly interesting in its coloration. The background, because it is multi-colored, yet darker than the model, adds depth and dimension to the painting.

Notice how masterfully and convincingly Shikler has managed to suggest depth and space between the model's right arm and the guitar in back of it. To create this illusion, the artist has first focused the strongest light on the curved hand, making it appear closest to the viewer's eye. Then he has subtly shaded and modeled the lower part of the forearm with a neutralizer, and then underscored this receding area with a very localized band of light, warm brown, which in turn rests on a deeply shadowed area. This carefully controlled series of shifts from light to dark creates the feeling of depth, space, and light between the model's knee and lap, as well as between her arm and the guitar.

Shikler has also been successful in suggesting—rather than actually showing—that the model is seated in a chair, although the only part of a chair visible is a hint of the arms peeking out from either side.

If Shikler finds that his drawing is inaccurate or weak in the final stage of a pastel painting, he does not hesitate to make necessary adjustments with charcoal, a procedure he refers to as "reinforcing his drawing," and one which he attributes to Degas. When the drawing is satisfactorily reinforced, he sprays it with fixative, then, if need be, strokes pastels over the charcoal to modify its harshness. *Woman with Guitar* is now complete.

20/Aaron Shikler
Paints a Female Figure

In this painting, *Woman Holding Cage*, it is interesting to keep in mind that both the model and the dress she is wearing are the same as in the previous demonstration done by Aaron Shikler—*Woman with Guitar*. Yet the two paintings, though they contain two identical major elements and are painted with very similar techniques, end up quite differently.

Phase one: the charcoal sketch

In this work (in contrast to the warm, soft, Venetian quality which suffuses *Woman with Guitar*), Shikler initially wanted to realize a cool, pale concept which he intended to develop with a cold, flat light that would rake over warmer colors and create sharp shadow effects.

The artist began by toning a pastel board with a casein wash of lavender. When this had dried, he decided that the tone was too pale and weak. He subsequently added a second wash, using a rich brown (burnt sienna) over the lavender. The combination of the warm and cool colors, he felt, would create a strong, dramatic backdrop for the statement of the figure he intended to paint over it.

Shikler then began to draw in charcoal over the toned board. Centering his figure on the board, he sketched her three-quarter view, with the arms extending toward the upper and lower corners and dominating the space all around them.

The artist has created an immediate impression of stretch, of graceful extension. He achieves this by his point of view. Note that he is not working on eye level with the model, but that he is looking up at her, and therefore drawing her at an angle which accentuates the ascending line of the torso and head. This line, moreover, rather than being rigidly upright, leans to the figure's left. Compositional balance is assured by the position of the arms, which stretch bird-like across and through the torso.

The artist, then, has filled his canvas with an x-like composition. Yet there is no feeling of rigidity in the drawing, for the subject itself—the female form—precludes it. The torso and head form a series of gentle curves whose sum is an arc beginning at the head and ending in the fold of the model's skirt. In the same way, the arms form a

---

Phase one. *The artist begins by making a charcoal drawing which not only defines forms, but lightly indicates the modeling. The features and hands are carried into further detail than the rest of the figure, since these represent the most complex drawing problems. The background has been toned with preliminary washes of lavender and burnt sienna which will subtly influence all the colors in the final painting.*

counter-arc to the body. Like looking at a cinerama screen, the viewer's eye, tunneling into the torso through the arched arms, receives the impression of depth.

If you compare the drawing stage of this pastel with the charcoal drawing of the previous demonstration, you will notice that while the first is the roughest, most minimal sketch, the second is a highly developed drawing, like a study for an old master painting. The torso and arms are not only placed and outlined, they are lightly modeled as well. The head is highly detailed: contours, features, hair are all precisely worked out in line and contour, with darks, middle values, and lights carefully placed. The hands, in particular, are carried into great detail, for they present the most challenging problems of foreshortening and perspective.

Phase two: the preliminary pastel

Because the artist carefully worked out all the problems of composition and drawing in the charcoal stage, and because he had a very clear idea of the color effects he wanted to achieve in pastel, he did not feel the need to undertake further preliminary experimentation. Shikler therefore skipped the casein underpainting stage and went directly into pastel.

It is significant that a certain amount of detail actually disappears in the second phase, in contrast to the charcoal drawing in the first phase. Note that the facial features are now simply patches of tone, the hair is a relatively flat tonal area, and the precise drawing of the hands begins to soften as the pastel is applied. At this stage, the artist is working for broad color areas and is consciously avoiding sharp edges, precise contours, and details which will distract him from seeing the painting as an organization of large shapes. When these broad shapes are established, he can then begin to "tighten up."

Emphasis is now placed on stating color harmonies and balance, and on developing textures. The background is scrubbed in. The model's hair is broadly developed with the side of the pastel, then lightly blended to eliminate individual strokes. In building up the flesh tones on the hands and face, Shikler has used green earth as a foundation and has slowly built up into burnt and raw umber halftones, blending with a stump or stroking with an umber neutralizer to modify and soften the effect. Juxtaposed and crosshatched strokes are visible on the neck and face.

Emphatic, Manet-like shadows underscore the outline of the waist, underarms, neck, and left shoulder of the figure. A lighter cast shadow has been placed along the right side of the skirt, while the folds once apparent on the left side of the skirt have been temporarily removed.

Shikler has begun to paint the brocade gown, shot through with silvery metallic threads, in cool tones of gray, moss green, and ultramarine blue. Black and neutralizer green are used for the shadows. The sleeves are built up in dark cadmium yellow,

---

Phase two. *Pastels are applied directly over the charcoal drawing, which virtually disappears beneath broad applications of color. Detail temporarily disappears in the face and hands, as well as in the cage. The modeling in the dress actually begins to flatten out in the upper torso, though a long shadow is introduced on the skirt. The darks of the hair and the insides of the arms and torso are strengthened. A background tone is scrubbed in.*

ochres, Naples yellow highlights, and burnt sienna shadows. A generous amount of black is blended into the gold sleeves. Shadows and contours on the face are developed with neutralizer green.

Phase three: finishing the pastel

In this stage, Shikler refines his drawing, adds details, and precisely distinguishes between textures and qualities of the various objects. The features of the face reappear delicately refined, with final highpoints of pinks and warm colors added to the nose, cheeks, lips, and ear. The hands and fingers have been developed in great detail, as have both the cage and the mouse. The hair, no longer a uniformly smooth, dark mass, shows individual strokes of ochre, dark cadmium yellow, and burnt siennas, which highlight and enliven this natural facial frame.

The rich and intricate brocade texture of the dress has been built up with techniques similar to the previous demonstration—by applying thousands of vigorous, irregular, yet highly controlled strokes of pastel, which are continually fixed, allowed to dry, then gone over in succeeding layers of pastel. The artist has carefully distinguished between the brocade of the dress and the satin of the cuffs; the mouse's fur and the woman's hair; the silver in the bells on the dress and collar of the mouse, and the brass of the cage.

Despite the high degree of finish, the painting sparkles because of this remarkable range of textures animating the entire surface. The rough, broken texture of the background (introduced in the second phase) is retained, although it is carried out in much smaller, more subtle strokes. Note how the background is built up with an enormous number of very free, broken strokes of warm and cool color which interlock and blend in the viewer's eye.

In contrast to the apparently random strokes of the background, notice the highly controlled network of directional strokes that move across the form of the head, rendering its roundness with precise draughtsmanship. Yet, upon close observation, one sees that the subtle tones of the head are not completely blended and ironed out into a continuous color, but are rather built up with a network of overlapping strokes which remain vibrant and crisp. The hair introduces a third kind of texture, with long rhythmic strokes that follow the direction of the hair. And the cuffs offer the equivalent of impasto —a thick buildup of light, intense color which draws the viewer's attention the way a thick passage of light paint would do in an oil painting. The effect is surprisingly like a painting by Vermeer, where one feels that the lights are built up with tiny chunks of pure color.

Color has been delicately balanced throughout the painting. What began as a pale work ends up dramatically rich and old masterish in tone. The tones of the back-

---

Phase three. *In the final phase, the hands and face are fully modeled; the cage and mouse are rendered completely, but the dress and background remain loosely handled. Note how the texture of the dress is actually made up of hundreds of free, broken strokes. Crisp notes of light, like impasto accents in oil painting, are thickly applied, giving an effect of remarkable freshness. The warm tone of the background is reflected in the shadows on the flesh tones, and the background itself contains subtle hints of the color tones of the dress.*

Detail of Woman Holding Cage *by Aaron Shikler.*

Woman Holding Cage *by Aaron Shikler, 40″ x 30″. Collection of the artist. Courtesy, Davis Galleries, New York.*

169

ground, itself a balance of warm and cool colors, are picked up and repeated elsewhere in the painting: in the rich brown of the woman's hair, and the burnt sienna shadows of the golden sleeves, for example. The dark cadmium yellow, ochre, and Naples yellow highlights which compose the sleeves are repeated in the tones of the cage, and hinted at in the body of the mouse. And the cool, blue-green of the dress is reiterated in the cool shadows of the flesh, which themselves play against warm, rosy highlights in the skin. This perfect balance and interplay of warm and cool, light and dark, busy and quiet, smooth and rough—achieved with almost awesome technical mastery—are the keys to the success of this superb painting.

Bibliography

Pastel Painting: Modern Techniques, by Stephan Csoka, Reinhold.

Pastels for Beginners, by Ernest Savage, Watson-Guptill.

Technique of Pastel Painting, by Leonard Richmond, Pitman.

Artist's Handbook of Materials and Techniques, by Ralph Mayer, Viking.

Color: A Complete Guide for Artists, by Ralph Fabri, Watson-Guptill.

Composition in Landscape and Still Life, by Ernest W. Watson, Watson-Guptill.

Drawing the Human Head, by Burne Hogarth, Watson-Guptill.

Drawing Lessons from the Great Masters, by Robert Beverly Hale, Watson-Guptill.

Dynamic Anatomy, by Burne Hogarth, Watson-Guptill.

How to Make Your Own Picture Frames, by Ed Reinhardt and Hal Rogers, Watson-Guptill.

Painting Lessons from the Great Masters, by Hereward Lester Cooke, Watson-Guptill.

Index

Edited by Judith A. Levy
Designed by James Craig
Composed in eleven point Baskerville monotype by Howard O. Bullard, Typographers
Printed and bound in Japan by Toppan Printing Co., Ltd.